Alan is foremost a healer who endeavours to help other people find their true path in life. He is a radio broadcaster, producing and hosting three radio shows each week.

He is also a theatre producer and psychic investigator.

To my partner, Anne, for her love and unwavering support.

Also, for my dear friend and Hollywood film producer Cyrus Yavneh, who sadly passed away on 25 January 2018. For my dear friend and Broadway producer Manny Fox, who sadly passed away on 23 September 2012.

You'll both forever be in our hearts.

Reverend Father Alan Cox

THE LIFE OF A PSYCHIC BROADCASTER

AUSTIN MACAULEY PUBLISHERS™

LONDON • CAMBRIDGE • NEW YORK • SHARJAH

A CIP catalogue record for this title is available from the British Library.

ISBN 9781788480420 (Paperback)
ISBN 9781788480437 (Hardback)
ISBN 9781528954143 (ePub e-book)

www.austinmacauley.com

First Published (2019)
Austin Macauley Publishers Ltd
25 Canada Square
Canary Wharf
London
E14 5LQ

To Cyrus Yavneh, David Parry, Sherrie Wilkolaski, Jesse Bravo and Jillian Haslam for their support and encouragement in writing this book.

Table of Contents

Preface

He spins around like a top. He sees ghosts in old buildings. He has visitations from Spirit Guides. He helps people whose beds levitate. Sounds fantastic? Far-fetched? Ridiculous? Not plausible?

But to Alan Cox, a real psychic healer, whose goal in life is to simply help people and earn an honest living for his family, these are unusual occurrences to be sure, but part of the job.

I thoroughly enjoyed reading Alan's biography; his voice is clear and unpretentious. It's okay to be sceptical, question, believe or not, but to Alan and Anne, it is honest and truthful; it is who they are.

His interviewees believe that they have seen apparitions, ghosts and guides. These are normal people who have experienced supernatural moments. It is as real to them as lunch. It doesn't make them excessive or unstable individuals. It is just the way it is for them.

To Alan and Anne, 'good' and 'evil' exist and are normal energies with corresponding suppliant entities. Guides, demons and the Devil are real. As you read the book, so much seems implausible, impossible, but that is their consciousness, their connection to Spirit.

Is it a curse or a blessing? I think if you would ask them, they would wholeheartedly say it is not only a blessing, it is their vocation and calling, and they are very humble with the responsibility of being intercessors with Spirit.

Alan is not on a soapbox. He is an ordinary, decent man, an intelligent man, a loving man, who wants nothing more than to use his gift for the good.

Enjoy the read. For those that are sceptics, ask yourself if you ever had an unexplained moment. For the people who understand and can relate, know you have found, in Alan, a kindred spirit.

To me the Spirit World Alan connects with, understands and shares, opens doors and windows, tears down walls, helps and allows, who he touches, to feel the spiritual sweet breeze of freedom that nourishes. Alan's gift is simply what it is. Nothing more, nothing less.

Cyrus Yavneh

Hollywood Producer/Director

Chapter 1
Early Years

Allow me to explain my wavelength. I was born on 28 March, 1950, into a loving family. That said, I am an only child. A boy brought up in a small town in Staffordshire, England, called Willenhall. Perhaps I should also mention my dad was named Sidney, while my mum was known as Frances. We lived with my Uncle Harry and Aunt Emily—whom I called Nan. Sadly, my mum's mum died giving birth to her in 1924. Moreover, my dad passed away in 1992, which was a very emotional time for me. Yet, thankfully, my mum, at the age of ninety-three, is still with us, albeit raised by her mum's sister, Emily. I recall people commenting she couldn't have children of her own. Perhaps, this was why my mum's dad didn't want to know her—so I hardly ever had contact with him. Looking back, I met him once while out shopping in Willenhall with my parents. Indeed, I remember it well—even down to the spot on the pavement outside a shop. I was about seven years old.

My mum said, "This is your granddad."

He gave me six pence. That was my single meeting with him. Later, I discovered he had remarried, and my mum had two stepbrothers, whom I have met twice, the last time at my dad's funeral. They seemed like decent chaps, but didn't get in touch afterwards. Overall, I took life as it came and didn't question what was happening.

In those days we lived on a main road on the edge of town. In the 1950s, common land was at the back of our house and we had beautiful views. Sadly it is all built up now with a large housing estate, taking up the mile of land, joining it to another housing estate. As memory has it, across the road were two old white-walled cottages where Uncle Harry's two sisters and brother lived. They owned the adjoining land, where lots of chickens were kept. Uncle Frank, who I never saw without wearing his old, battered, dark brown trilby hat, had an old-fashioned workshop with a wood-burning heater in the centre. To my recollection, a flue went up and out of the roof. I loved being there in the winter, when it was cold outside but roasting inside.

A canal ran alongside the far end of this triangle-shaped piece of land, each territory allowing rats to come up from the bank and terrorise these chickens, events after which my pet dog, 'Spot' (so called because of a white spot on the end of his tail and one on his tummy), would be summoned to kill the rats. He loved this adventure and proved extremely quick and efficient in dispatching them to rat heaven, the only problem being that he needed to be stopped from jumping up and licking people's faces once he had finished—an unpleasant happening I experienced a few times.

Other difficulties included an occasion when Uncle Frank said to me, "Have you ever seen a dead chicken run?"

By way of a reply, I said, "No."

Thereupon, he promptly caught hold of one and chopped its head off. Shockingly, the chicken ran headless around the yard with blood spewing out all over the place—until its nervous system failed. Obviously, this upset me a lot. Somewhat shocked, my uncle was himself mortified that he had upset me. Yet, I can see now that it was the 'bad energies' at work. Nonetheless, this idyllic time in my life started to come to a close when, one by one, my aunts and uncles died. Remembered so, the most traumatic passing for me being when Uncle Harry left our mortal coil. At the time, I was 13, and it had a big effect on me. Albeit, years earlier, Harry had become ill with gangrene. Threateningly, his condition required his left leg to be amputated above the knee—in the vain hope of stopping it spreading throughout his body. Initially, of course, he recovered well and even had an artificial leg fitted. Equipment, in those days, consisting of a metal frame, hinged at the knee, along with a wooden club on the end acting as the foot. Curiously, he mastered it and could get a move on. It didn't stop him doing what he wanted to and, eventually, I got used to seeing him without his leg. However, the fittings then were very poor, and he would have sores on the stump.

All things considered, my uncle was a very keen gardener. He carried on gardening even though it was hard for him. I used to help him sow vegetable seeds. His garden was 150-feet long and very wide. At the bottom-right hand side of the garden, he had a greenhouse in which he would grow tomatoes and cucumbers. There were two long lawns on either side of a central pathway. The garden was lower than his house; the ground dropped away by about 10 feet beyond the patio area. On the left-hand side of his house, there was a metal shed, housing all of his bicycles, a lawn mower and a sundry of tools. Additionally, there was a narrow gap at the back of the shed, although it couldn't be seen from the house. To my child's mind, I thought I could get away with jumping down to the large vegetable patch (unseen) and eat the peas I loved. It's strange how a child's mind works! I thought if I shelled the peas while they were still attached to the plant, no one would be any wiser.

Occasionally, I would hear my Uncle Harry call out, "He's been at the peas again!" Then, he would laugh and say, "Wait until dinnertime; we won't have any left at the rate you eat them."

So this was my life; no great issues. I wasn't spoilt, but I never went without anything. I always felt loved.

School life was a bit of a challenge for me. I just couldn't grasp most subjects. What is more, being a quiet person, I unfortunately attracted bullies. This is how I found out how strong I really was. Two brothers in my class said they would beat me up if I didn't hand over my pocket money each week. This went on for approximately three weeks. Thence, demanded more. I thought enough was enough.

I remember standing in front of them in the playground and saying to them, "You are not going to get a penny more from me, so beat me up if you are going to."

They looked at me, then at each other, and walked away. They never bothered me again. They didn't even acknowledge me from that time on, which suited me fine.

I kept a lot to myself, not confiding in anyone, even though I didn't know why I was always frightened at bedtime.

After my nan and uncle had passed away (my uncle only outliving Nan by 12 months), I moved from my small box-bedroom into the large front bedroom that was my uncle and aunt's. I remember their old style metal-framed bed with its large coiled open springs and tall dark wooden headboard. Its short footboard doubled up as the legs. On its top, there was a cosy feather mattress. Yet, I dreaded going to bed at night and had to have the bedroom door open and the landing light on. In itself, the bed was situated behind the door, and I would stare in fear of something—I don't know what—coming into the room. Every night I would have to check under the bed in case someone was hiding there. In hindsight, I can see that bad forces in spirit were working on me. I know now that the devil knew I would one day be able to help people in a psychic-spiritual way and he wanted to stop this from happening.

When I was 13, I had a suspected infected appendix. Hence, a doctor was called for me. I remember it being a Saturday morning and I was in a lot of pain. Following his examination, the physician, Doctor Pottinger, said I needed to go to hospital and duly called an ambulance to take me there. I wanted to be in my parents' bedroom, so I waited there by myself with my parents downstairs. I was terrified. While in the quiet of the room, I heard a deep, growling voice loudly saying it was going to get me. I screamed out, and my mum and dad came running upstairs to see what was happening. I explained. They said I must have been having a bad dream and there was nothing to worry about. I didn't argue with them. I knew I hadn't been dreaming; I was wide awake at the time and I was in too much pain to sleep. So, the thought of going to hospital was horrifying. Up until then, I had never been away from my parents. I was kept in the Manor Hospital in Walsall for three days, as a precaution. They did that back then. Today, patients are in and out so quickly, they hardly have time to put on their pyjamas. Fortunately, no operation was needed. Indeed, the doctors couldn't understand why I was in so much pain. When the pain stopped they sent me home.

The next incident that has stayed etched in my mind is the time when I played football by myself at the front of the house. These houses were way back from the street and gave me room to play. Thus, I pretended to be a member of my favourite football team, Wolverhampton Wanderers (the Wolves). One day, a man walked down the road, stopped, and asked how he could get to the towpath of the canal. He said he wanted to walk to Walsall. Respectfully, I pointed to the entrance to the towpath. It was plain to see.

He then said, "Come and show me."

Fearfully, I ran to the nearest house and knocked frantically on the door. Mrs Gardiner opened the door, whilst this stranger ran down the road and disappeared near the canal. I could see I was becoming a repeated target for the devil.

The next significant event took place one Sunday morning in summer. I remember being in the back garden, as a young man came out of our back door and walked up to me. He was holding a crystal pendulum.

He said, "Look at this, Alan."

I said, "What is it?" as I observed a silver chain with a dark brown crystal hanging beneath it.

Interestingly, there were beautiful markings in it. Suddenly, it started to quickly go round in a circles. However, I could see he was not making it move. His hand, wrist and arm were still at the same place as it was spinning at great speed. I was mesmerised and enthralled by what was happening. It stopped after a few minutes.

This caused me to say to the man, "How did you do that?"

He looked at me with a gentle smile on his face, "You will find out one day."

I remember him turning away from me and going back into the house as I carried on playing in the garden. Bemused, I tried to understand what had gone on. Oddly, that stated, I didn't mention what had happened to my parents. The next day at school, I kept thinking about what had gone on the day before, so when I returned home, I asked my mum who had visited us that Sunday morning. Astonishingly, she said no one had visited and asked why I thought someone had come around. I said I thought I had seen a man in the house through the window. She said I was mistaken. Obviously, I knew our back garden was completely enclosed—with no way into it other than through the house. Eventually, I put it to the back of my mind, because I couldn't think of a logical explanation for this event. Whoever it was, he was right. I have found out all about it. Currently, I use a pendulum virtually every day to link in to spirit and help others.

I can remember looking up to the sky at night, seeing the stars and saying to myself, "You are protected, you will always be safe."

When all was said and done, I felt I was being looked after by an unseen force.

Of course, the time came for me (at the age of 16) to leave school and join the adult world of working. In 1966, however, it was a totally different working world from today. It was really easy to find a job. I remember the career officers coming to our school. All the school-leavers, including myself, were herded into the main hall. It was a big school, covering a large catchment area—Willenhall Comprehensive needed to find jobs for a huge number of pupils. Regardless, my turn duly came and I was asked what I wanted to do.

I replied without hesitation, "I want to help people."

Without blinking an eye, the career officer retorted, "There is a vacancy in Walsall at the Co-op Departmental Store in the furniture department to train as a salesman. That's helping people to choose what they want to buy."

Immediately, I was given an official form with my appointment for the interview. The next day, I went along and, after five minutes with the manager, was given a job.

For me, this was the start of adulthood. I forgot all about happenings from before and entered a world of work and girls. Oh yes, this was the start of me finding out about them. I fell in love with every girl I fancied and dated! I was very naive to begin with.

In the UK, one needs to be 17 to drive a car. Although by 16 it is permitted to ride a moped. As such, I was determined to be mobile. So, I bought a moped for £25.00 and applied for a provisional driving licence. This was the beginning of my independence. However, I didn't take my motorbike test until I was 17, when I sent for my provisional car driving licence. Thence, I had my first lesson two days following my birthday. Eleven lessons later (accompanied by a lot of practice in my dad's car), I passed my driving test on the first attempt. That was it! I got rid of my moped and bought my first car for

£50.00. It was a light blue two-door vehicle, three speeds—a very old Ford Popular. It had spring seats, with a spring sticking out through the fabric of the driver's seat, close to the edge where one got in. Obviously, I snagged a lot of trousers. Now, a 17-year-old with his own car in 1967, in England, was a rarity, making me a popular person. It also helped me advance in my occupation quickly. After all, being mobile, I was a great asset to the company I worked for. Additionally, I made the most of my independence by travelling all over the UK, always with my latest girlfriend in tow. That was until I met Irene, my wife to be.

Speaking of compatible wavelengths, my friend, Martin Folan, and I had booked a two-week holiday driving across Europe: taking in France, Switzerland, Lichtenstein, Austria and Italy. Just two weeks before we went, I met Irene. We hit it off straight away. Unquestionably, it was quite emotional leaving her, even though she said she would wait for me to return. Nonetheless, the holiday was great fun, albeit my mind was back in England looking forward to seeing her again. As soon as I returned, I took her away to Wales for the weekend and asked her to marry me. She said yes, and we were married just four months later.

My early years were well and truly over and life altered completely.

Chapter 2
My Ordinary Time

Overall, the frequency had changed radically. Explaining, perhaps, when I was 18 I had an overwhelming dread of being fifty. It seemed totally irrational, yet completely consuming. For months on end, this fear was with me night and day. Not a fear of getting old, nor a fear of death. Instead, it was fear of the unknown. I sensed something was going to happen that would have an impact on my life, big time, but what? I tried to put it to the back of my mind and got on with my life. However, these thoughts were never far away.

Eventually, it happened, And how? Curiously, it took me 32 years to find out the reason behind this anxiety. A phobia revealed later on the dot. Confessed so, everything will be revealed as this story unfolds.

Getting back to my teens, I left the Co-op and moved to Sidney Brown's upmarket furniture store in Walsall. I was 18, working hard and playing hard. It was 1968—exciting times to be a teenager. In those days, weekends consisted of going to top nightclubs in Birmingham. Even the name of the clubs sounded exciting to an 18-year-old: 'Barbarella's', 'Dolcivita', 'The Tower', 'Rebecca's'.

As for working, the staff at the store were great people. All, except for the manager who was full of himself. Personally, I was good friends with three of the salesmen. Particularly, Dave Palmer, who was the oldest at 32. He was a rebel trying to be normal and had been in a number of pop groups, including 'Screaming Lord Sutch', as well as 'The Savages'. Oddly, he left the former group after being set-alight on stage by 'Screaming Lord Sutch'. Escaping injury, thank heavens, with just minor burns. Interestingly, he had grown up with people who later became famous. Some were really good friends of his, another reason for hanging around with him and his wife, Barbara. Unsurprisingly, the parties were wild. So stated, I never took drugs. It wasn't my thing, even though there were plenty on offer.

Fascinatingly, Dave's good friend was Roy Woods—the Debenhams Department Store on Broad Street Birmingham lead singer with 'The Move' and later on 'Wizzard' pop groups. He was great fun, just as wild as he was on stage. I remember one day over the others. I was with Dave and Barbara in.

We were quite close to the entrance when Roy came into the store, saw us, and shouted at the top of his voice, "Dave."

Obviously, there were quite a few shoppers in there. All meaning, everyone turned to see what was going on. He created a commotion wherever he went.

In themselves, weekends were for partying and clubbing. I would be out all night every Saturday, giving my parents sleepless nights, since they were worried if I was alright. In hindsight, this wasn't good. I was trying to find my own way in life, away from the confines of being an only child.

Each, a factor leading my recollections back to the time when I met my first wife Irene. Notably, not through Dave, but from work. Indeed, we met in the July of 1972 and had a whirlwind romance, marrying in the December of that same year.

I was working at the furniture store in Wolverhampton when this beautiful girl, with very long dark hair, came into the shop to buy a leg for a divan base. She had been sent by her boss—although actually working as a waitress two doors down at an Italian restaurant. Instantly, I was taken with her. Henceforth, it became my mission to have a date with her. To be honest, I have never liked Italian food very much, but every lunchtime for a week, I went to the restaurant until I had forged a good relationship with her and could ask her out. That was it; we were an item as they say.

Three children and 15 years later, the marriage came to an end. I was devastated. Irene had cheated on me. Yet, I was still in love with her. Looking back, I can see now that the relationship was meant to finish. However, I will always love her for giving me my wonderful boys, whom in turn have given me beautiful grandchildren.

The divorce was complete in 1987. I had two years of being single again before meeting Anne.

I didn't know it then, but this was the way Spirit would wake me up to the psychic world.

Chapter 3
Awakening

In 1992, one of the darkest times for me was of my father passing away. It took me a long time to come to terms with this event. I used to, and still do, talk to him in my mind. I find a lot of comfort in this. He also visits me in spirit and often joins Anne and myself in the car, usually sitting on the back seat with my daughter, who is also in spirit. Unarguably, Caroline, my daughter, plays with my hair whilst I am driving. I can feel her wrapping my hair around her finger. However, if I look in the mirror, my hair isn't moving. It makes me smile. Admittedly, I have omitted any writings about Caroline. It is simply too painful for me to go into how we lost her. This was the darkest of my dark hours.

Acknowledged so, in 1996, events happened that changed both my life and Anne's forever. I had moved in to live with her four years earlier—on the Christmas of the year my father died. Indeed, I recall us making plans for the future together, when strange things started to happen at home.

Clearly, Anne had always been a positive person, even though this changed. At the time, we both put it down to the start of the menopause. Men make jokes about it, but there isn't much to laugh about. It seems to me to be a cruel thing that most women experience. Menopause makes women even more sensitive than they generally are. Whether this had bearing on what was about to happen, can only be speculated upon. That said, I think it did.

One case immediately comes to mind.

I was at work while Anne was alone at home. It was the middle of the day. Now, her account of the event that happened was that she had gone upstairs into the bedroom and felt the need to lie down. After about thirty minutes, she woke with a start and went to go downstairs. Taking merely one step down the staircase, she felt a hard push on her back, which caused her to lose her balance. Instinctively, she reached out with her right hand to grab the banister rail; it came away in her hand. She was sent gambolling down the stairs—narrowly missing the telephone table in the hallway. Anne realised she had broken her wrist; although she felt no pain. Instantly, she got a bag of frozen peas out of the freezer to help minimise the swelling. Thus, I arrived at home from work just before seven in the evening to find Anne sitting on the bottom step nursing her wrist. So, off to hospital we went to get Anne's wrist set and plastered.

A few days later, Anne and I were watching television. A new series had started called 'House Busters', wherein psychics would go into people's homes if they were having similar problems as ours. We saw Dave Ashworth on the show and intuitively knew he was the person to help us. As such, I called Channel 5 TV. Kindly, they forwarded my contact details to David. He called us a few days later and made arrangements to come to our home to do a spiritual cleansing. Little did I know that this was the start of my spiritual awakening!

The following week I called Dave. He invited Anne and me to his home in Manchester. I recall it being a lovely summer's day in June. Oh yes, we do have nice weather in England and it doesn't always rain in Manchester.

Dave suggested we spend some time in the back garden, so with Dave's partner, Denise, we all went outside. We stood there talking.

Suddenly, Dave turned to me and said, "Hold this medal in your left hand," which I duly did.

He said it had been charged with the power of the Archangel Gabriel. I had no idea what he meant. In addition, Dave told me that my spirit guide was called Ronaldo—who had lived over 400 years ago in Brazil. Significantly, Dave spoke to me as if he was reading out a letter from Ronaldo. He said that Ronaldo and I had a lifetime of work to do together, and he would contact me in a few days. I was totally bewildered, but intrigued by this statement. Then something monumental happened.

Dave said, "Hold the medal in your left hand and ask Ronaldo to show you, yes."

I said in reply, "What do you mean?"

Dave responded, "By asking, you will be shown, yes."

Well, what happened next was mind-blowing. I asked Ronaldo to show me 'yes', after which I started to rotate. Astonishingly, my whole body—from top to toe—started to go round in an anti-clockwise direction, starting slowly, then gaining speed until I was spinning like a top. Strangely, I did not lose balance. Instead, I was pivoting on the balls and heels of my feet (I have consciously tried to do this many times since, but it can't be done).

To this day, I can hear Dave, Denise and Anne saying, "What's going on?" and "That's impossible!"

However, I must not digress.

I then heard Dave say, "Ask Ronaldo to stop!"

I asked this repeatedly even though it seemed to take forever. Eventually, of course, I did stop.

Dave then said, "Ask Ronaldo to show you, no." Obviously, I did, and I started to spin in a clockwise direction, just as fast as before.

I then said to Ronaldo "Stop!" and, immediately, came to a standstill. Neither time did I lose my balance! Afterwards, I just stood there quiet and motionless. I felt no dizziness, just confusion as to what had gone on. Dave said he was guided to get me to do this, even though he had never before witnessed anything like it.

Three days later, just as Ronaldo had said, he filled my head with thoughts of a kind I had never had before.

The predominant concept was that I could heal. Also, I came to understand I could clear bad energies from people and places. I noticed my hands, simultaneously, went red hot: they glowed. Yet, I wasn't given much time for all of this to sink in. Anne and I needed to visit Clive, her brother, and his wife, Lynne, a few days after this happened. Obviously, what had gone on was the main topic of conversation.

Lynne kept horses at a livery stable and found herself (the next day) talking about me to one of the other women who additionally kept a horse at the stables. Perhaps, coincidentally, the woman said that her brother was going through a really bad time at home. She added he was in his early twenties and lived with his parents. They were very worried about him. Unsurprisingly, I was asked if I could help him. I then discovered that her brother was occasionally thrown out of his bed at night by an unseen force. He had even been pushed against a wardrobe in his bedroom, while this wardrobe had been pushed over on another occasion.

I said I would help if I could. There was no hesitation on my part. I felt no fear, or apprehension, about going to his home. I felt the strength of Ronaldo was with me.

So, my first spiritual work was to clear and free this family of the living nightmare that had been going on for years. Although the ghostly goings on were happening in the bedroom, I found the demon hiding in their cellar. I felt its presence and there was a horrendous smell of rotten cabbages, which I later found out, was a demonic signature.

I promptly got to work. Using my dowser pendulum, I linked in with the help of Ronaldo to clear this unwanted presence. The dowser spun round clockwise at speed—just as I myself had at David's home. I saw, in my third eye, this revolting creature being drawn to a bright light. My guide (and others Ronaldo had enlisted to help) was dragging it into the light. The demon then entered the light, which closed up like a trap door never to return.

David had given me this pendulum dowser, saying I would need it. He was so right.

The family had no further problems of that nature. Job done. What an introduction to the world of spirit. I felt a warm glow inside me, as if I were being told I would be helping a lot more people over the coming years. I thanked Ronaldo and the other guides for their help. After all, we were in partnership. He couldn't do the work without my energy, and I couldn't do it without the spirit guides' energies.

The next experience was only a few days later. Word about what was happening began to spread quickly. Fred, Anne's dad, had told his neighbours. Hence, the next time we visited Fred, one of his neighbours came round to ask if I could help her brother. At that time he was visiting her. He had colitis, but was frightened to go to a doctor. Hearing this, I went round to see him. I said, "Look, I am not medically qualified and have no idea if I can help. You really should go and see a doctor."

Replying, he said, "I understand that, but it can't do any harm by you just putting your hands on me." Moments later, I was guided to hold his left arm, which prompted him to say, "The problem isn't there, Alan."

I said, "I know, but that is where I need to touch you."

Well, the next thing that happened was he felt a massive clearing, healing, and energy from the troubled area. It was like a great release, he said. The energy travelled up and round to his left arm, where my hand was. Personally, I felt it enter my hand and leave from the back of my hand. From then onwards, he had no further problem.

I do not take any credit for this happening. I know and understand it was God's energy flowing through me. Overall, I am used as a conduit to achieve these positive results.

With all this happening, I was confused as to what I was doing with my life. What is more, I was frustrated and unsettled in my job. Truly, I had always been restless where work was concerned, although I had never been out of work and always looked to advance myself with better paid jobs. I had been a salesman all my adult life. This time, however, things were different. I was looking for something, but didn't understand what it could be. Moreover, I saw people in a different way. Obviously, I have never been judgmental and have always seen other people's point of view. These events were almost allowing me see into their minds, even into their souls. In a sense, I could harmonise with their vibrations and tune into their frequencies. At work, I could virtually see into the hypocrisy of colleagues' words and actions. Therefore, I changed my job three times in as many years. All in all, I was good at what I did and never had a problem being employed. That said, each new position didn't satisfy me, even though sales were always improving. I thought to myself, *What is the point of making shareholders richer? I am all for free enterprise, but these things didn't seem important to me anymore.*

By this time, I had reached my 50th birthday. An occasion when I knew I couldn't stand working for anyone else anymore. Looking back, a lot of my work had been self-employed but always as an agent having to follow other people's rules. I needed my freedom.

I had no great amount of money saved. I had always (in hindsight) foolishly spent what I had. Saving didn't seem relevant. To my mind, I would always have plenty of money, because I always earned plenty of money. Nonetheless, I was in for a rude awakening.

I started my own one-man sales business. During the week, I travelled the length and breadth of the British Isles, selling dart equipment to public houses and social clubs. I was away from home every day, which meant I had to cram being with Anne and spending time with my children into weekends—at the same time as restocking for the week ahead. One of these weekends, Anne said she wanted to go to a psychic event, advertised locally. She thought it would help us both. Uncannily, this turned out to be a major turning point in both of our lives.

Hence, we went along to the event. Neither of us knew what we were doing there. It was strange! We knew we were meant to be there, but why? Neither of us had had a reading from any clairvoyants, ever, although all of this was about to change. One of the clairvoyants got up from his table for a break.

He walked past us and unexpectedly said to me, "You will be doing this one day."

I was stunned. We left after having been there only 10 minutes. On the way out, I picked up a leaflet with the organiser's name and contact details on it. For no apparent reason, I said to Anne that we should buy crystals and jewellery and sell them at events like this. Anne agreed! So, I sourced wholesalers, and the following week, we had bought a load of stock. I never did do things by halves; 'Straight in there' was my motto.

Being logical, I got in touch with the organiser of the psychic event we had attended. He said we could sell our crystals etc. at his events. Following this beginning, we did likewise every weekend at different locations up and down the country. As an enterprise, we were doing reasonably well.

At one of these events in Bristol, the same clairvoyant was present.

He came over to me and said, "My name is Michael Smith. My wife Lesley and I are putting on our own event. You need to be there and give spiritual readings to people."

I immediately responded, "Yes."

Personally, I was excited and nervous, even though Anne and I went along. For her part, Anne sold her crystals, while I had an empty table with no tablecloth, sign or tarot cards. I only had my dowser pendulum. Thus, when the event opened at 1 pm, I kept as far away from my table as possible. I was too nervous to sit there in case someone came up and asked me for a reading. However, there was no hiding place.

Lesley came up to me and said, "There is a lady over there who wants a reading from you."

Unnoticed to me, Lesley had been talking to a lady who asked whom she ought to go to for a reading. Lesley had thrown me in at the deep end. This was going to be my first ever reading given to anyone. I had had no practice; no dummy runs with family or friends; this was it.

Eventually, this lady and I took our positions at the table; I forgot all about the dowser pendulum in my pocket. I looked her in the eye and then information began to pour from my mouth. I had no control over what I was saying.

This is as close as I can remember to the words exchanged.

I said, "You have always wanted to start up your own business, but your husband has always said you can't afford to. You can, but he doesn't want you to; you are both well off. Yet, that isn't why you are here. He has been having an affair with your best friend who is also your next door neighbour. You will be moving home. However, it will be only temporary. You will be moving again very shortly. You have made the right decision."

She looked at me in amazement, then a big smile came over her face.

Afterwards, she said to me, "You are right; we could afford to set up a shop for me to own and run," she continued, "thank you, Alan. Yes, I have just found out about their affair. Additionally, I have been into estate agents and put down a deposit on an empty house. A decision based on the pictures they were advertising. You are right, it will only be temporally; I just have to get away from them both." She got up from her chair with a smile still on her face, "I know I am doing the correct thing, thank you again." The lady left this session with a spring in her step, while I knew it was Spirit's way of introducing me to my psychic wavelength. If I had any doubts beforehand, they were now gone.

My awakening was complete. What was to follow over the coming years proved even more remarkable!

Chapter 4
The House from Hell

I bought her ex-husband's share of the house she had purchased with him. Clearly, she wanted us to have a fresh start with a house that would have no connection with him. Now, don't get me wrong. Anne and I got on well with Jim, not to mention the fact that their son, Lee, and I get on really well with each other. Hence, no distancing was needed from either side. Instead, we wanted to create a new home together.

Fortunately, we had first time buyers, so there was no chance to hold up the sale. Furthermore, we decided to move in with Anne's mum and dad in order for the sale to go through quickly. After five months of sharing their home, we moved into our new house from hell.

Now you might rightly ask why we didn't realise that this house was going to be a nightmare. A reasonable question answered by the fact that we were completely hoodwinked! After all, a dentist can't pull his own tooth out. Rather, he needs to get treatment from another dentist. In which case, the same is true for a psychic. We didn't ask for help, so we had a big lesson to learn.

Following our move, everything started to go wrong. Even my sales dropped dramatically, making it hard to live properly. We just kept our heads above water. Also, my car and Lee's car were vandalised on the drive of our house; my car had tar poured over it. Then a week later, Lee's rear car window had a house brick put through it. The next thing that happened was, I began to see (in my third eye), blood running down the back wall of the living room. However, after researching the area, I found that the house was on an estate built upon a small hill in West Bromwich. Indeed, it had been constructed in the early 1970s on land reclaimed from mining. Thence, two and two started to make four. These disused mine shafts below the estate had witnessed men die while extracting coal many years previously. Unsurprisingly, therefore, we heard noises coming from different rooms when Anne and I were in the same room with no one else in the house.

During this time, Lee had a car and, at the age of 18, was finding his way in the world. He had left school and was doing an apprenticeship with BT. As it goes, he still works for them as a top manager in their organization. Moreover, he had met a woman 11 years older than himself, who had a 9-year-old daughter. This woman saw Lee as her solution for a secure future. In himself, Lee wouldn't listen to anyone and duly left home to live with her. This was in the January of 2001. As one can imagine, Anne was beside herself with worry, thinking Lee was going to ruin his life. All meaning that every time Anne saw Lee, they would clash and Lee would storm off. By the time January was coming to an end, Lee had stopped visiting us.

This made Anne think she had lost him for good. I told her to try and not get anxious, because he would be back by the end of June that year. As if by magic, a week later (we were driving North on the M6 motorway and had just passed the exit for junction 11, which is close to our present home), a dirty white transit van moved ahead us. Unbelievably, scrawled in its dirt, was the name Natalie, the name of the girl Lee was partnering!

Instantly, Anne commented, "That's some kind of a message for us, but what does it mean?"

It took another two days before it came to me. What happens to dirty vans? Eventually they are cleaned and all the dirt is gone; so Natalie will go from our lives.

The months went by until the 30th June came round prompting Anne to state, "You were wrong. Lee hasn't come back and he will be lost forever."

For some reason or other, I didn't answer. That evening, I had six readings to do at a house a mile away from where we lived. Customarily, I turned my mobile phone off. However, at exactly 8 pm, in the middle of one of the readings, my phone rang. I apologised to my client and asked if I could interrupt the reading to answer it as I could see it was Anne calling.

Straightaway, Anne said, "He's back. Lee's back. He said to me that you and I were right!" Lee then ran upstairs and shut himself in his room.

Spirit was right, of course. Lee was going to come back home all the time. We just had to let him learn his lesson. Lee is now very happily married to Leanne. They have two sons, Zachary and Phoenix.

Nevertheless, we started to look for another house and after 20 months moved to where we are now. Unsurprisingly, when the time came to move, we had some of the worst experiences ever. Indeed, we were fortunate that Clive (Anne's brother who works as a driver for a haulage firm) asked if he could borrow one of their 750-tonne vans to move our furniture. Amazingly, they said yes—at no cost! So, Clive, Anne, their dad, Fred and I set about moving the contents of the house, which was a ten mile journey. As for the new occupiers of our old house, they were not moving in for another week. All implying, we had plenty of time to move. In the long run, it was a good job we did. It was if the house was trying to hold on to us. It took forever to load items into the van and ages to unload at the other end for no apparent reason. Altogether, it took three days to move everything from a three-bedroom semi-detached house to another three-bedroomed house. On Monday, the day after the completion of the move, I remembered that I had forgotten something at the old house. Fortunately, Lee had forgotten to hand in his front door key. So back I went to retrieve the item.

However, I went there by myself. As I opened the front door—the main hall was to the left of the stairs which were facing me about three feet into the house—my eyes were drawn to the top of the stairs. A place where I saw a standing woman dressed in 1920s style working class clothes looking down at me. I froze and just stared at her. The woman looked as solid as I was. Her greying hair tied back in a bun, which was usual for that era. I would say she was about 40 years old and looked worn-out. Factors indicating she had lived a tough life in our dimension. Slightly shocked, it seemed an eternity that I stood at the bottom of those stairs. In reality, it was about 30 seconds or so. Following this, she turned around and walked through the wall behind her. To my recollection, it was the wall into the bathroom. Now, I clear ghosts as part of my daily life, but I will admit I wasn't expecting anything like this to happen. I was spooked, if you will excuse the pun. Extremely quickly, therefore, I retrieved the item I had come for and let myself out. Once clear, I locked the outside door and posted the key back into the house through its letterbox. Thusly, the house was completely empty of all our personal belongings. Happenings making me realise some buildings are very hard to clear. A common occurrence, dare I say, when there is a direct connection to the underworld. Undoubtedly, that house had been built on very unsettled land. Indeed, if I think of our time living there, we had lovely neighbours, yet they were all going through bad times, including ill health. Stated so, it does not really matter where one lives, since 99% of buildings can be cleared of bad energies. The 1% that can't is due to the fact it's like trying to empty water out of a rowing boat with a hole in the bottom of it, a clear impossibility.

Be that as it may, we had moved. Now (12 plus years later), we are happy. Overall, it seems human beings are meant to experience these things in order to understand what other people go through. Hence, I am more or less sure our spirit guides will confirm these things when the time to move again comes. Uncannily, I feel we will be moving in the future.

Chapter 5
Radio

I had been asking God and my spirit guides to allow me to become better known. Not for the sake of fame, but to be able to share my knowledge of Spirit with as many people as possible, so that others could judge for themselves concerning the relevance of Spirit in their own lives. Also, perhaps, for them to have a greater understanding of the events that they have experienced.

As such, I received an email from a man in America named Craig Eugene. He said he had been surfing the internet for possible hosts for an online spiritual radio station he had joined, his remit being to recruit suitable people.

Straight away, I replied saying, "Yes, I would love to." And that was the beginning of my radio-hosting career as well as the start of a great friendship with Craig—a relationship continuing until today.

Unsurprisingly, he has been a regular guest on my show over the years, and I have been a guest on his show many times in return. Stated so, Craig is a renowned psychic-medium who lives in Pennsylvania, USA—a gentleman who gave me the confidence and supports that has led me to interview famous people from all walks of life, including authors, singers, and Broadway-stage and Hollywood-film producers. Every one of which has an interest, or connection, with Spirit and the paranormal. However, I will talk about the incredible people I have interviewed, some whom have become good friends of mine, until later in this extended essay.

Nonetheless, during one of our regular chats on the phone, Craig told me of an unusual client who came to him for help. The client mentioned that after losing a loved one, she had gone to a so-called psychic who had (systematically over a period of around two months) taken over five thousand dollars from her and did nothing to help her.

Furthermore, all of the alleged information he had given she knew to be false. Obviously, Craig helped her, but was so incensed by what had gone on that he wanted to expose this rogue psychic. He asked me if we could join forces and broadcast a radio show together on this topic. Agreeing, we eventually went live on-air together and exposed a number of psychics as charlatans.

We took it in turns to phone different psychics to catch them out. We prepared beforehand by surfing the internet for websites that could be suspect. Clearly, there was a running theme going through certain types of websites—the type of websites that promised to bring lovers back together even if one of the people didn't want to be with the other one anymore—by putting a love spell on them.

I found one such site. This person said in her write-up that she could do it. Stereotypically, there was no address, just an American phone number, which I found out was from the Chicago area, along with an email address. I called her live on-air. She seemed a very kind and plausible person, so it was easy to see how a vulnerable person could be taken-in.

Anyway, I had already made up a false story about myself. None of the main facts were true, although I began by using my real name. I told her how I had lost the woman I loved. Also, I told her I was calling from England which was true. Adding I had found her website and felt drawn to her for help. She listened intensely to what I had to say. The story being, a year earlier, I had met an American girl who was working and living in London, saying we had been together all that time before she left me and went back to New York.

I said her name was Mary and I couldn't live without her. Then, the 'psychic' said I should hold on the phone, while she made contact psychically with Mary. After about one minute, she came back on the phone saying she had linked into Mary (the Mary who didn't exist) and had picked up that she regretted leaving me, but was too frightened to get back in touch with me because she knew how much she had hurt me and let had me down. This 'psychic' continued to say that if I paid her five hundred dollars, she would cast a spell that would get Mary to return to me, since we were meant to be together.

Responding, I said, "Before I pay you the money, there is something I need to explain to you." In anticipation, she asked me what this was. Following which, I explained, "My name is Alan Cox. I am calling you from England. Mary is a figment of my imagination, so how can you get her to come back to me if she doesn't exist? Oh, and by the way, you are on live internet radio with people listening to you from all over the world." Threateningly, she said karma would come back on me, and that I was a terrible person to trick her in this way. Immediately, she then hung the phone up.

Obviously, I told my listeners the website address to prevent anyone in a vulnerable condition calling this person. Unfortunately, there are unscrupulous people in this world, who would rather take from people than help them.

Let me stress, we are all human and no psychic can get everything right all of the time, but to deliberately try to deceive in order to get money is evil in my book.

Nevertheless, my radio career had started with a bang, and it has grown over the years. In fact, I cherish my ability to connect with people from all over the world. What is more, radio has allowed me to assist people through passing on information, or directly going to their houses to clear bad energies from their homes and work places.

Chapter 6
Paramania Networking

In 2010, I spent a year presenting my '*Understanding Spirit*' radio show on Para X Radio. During this time my confidence grew, aided, of course, by 'behind the scenes' people like Dave Erickson. Indeed, I got to know him through Craig Eugene who was also at the radio station. On one occasion, during a three-way Skype phone call, Dave said he and his wife, Jennifer Stewart, had for a long time wanted to have their own internet radio station. Moreover, after years of wishing for it, they were about to launch it. The name was going to be '*Paramania Radio*'. Dave didn't ask Craig or me to join him on his new station. He is the type of guy who wouldn't try to poach anyone. However, after listening to him, I instantly said I would like to host my show on his new network. Thus, I became his first recruit, although getting the radio station up and running was not going to be plain sailing.

Ominously, Dave and Jenny lived in Maryland, in a house possessed by more than one evil spirit. Realising the gravity of their situation (and since they had decided to go ahead with their new radio station), these negative ghostly activities increased to a point they felt threatened. Dave described it as another 'House from Hell'.

Certainly, the whole family experienced blood running down its walls, as well as sensing disembodied spirits walking around the house. Astonishingly, one by one, each of them underwent a physical attack at any time of day. In the end, the whole family left the house because it was too hard to cope with. Unsurprisingly, now the house is up for sale, it still hasn't sold following two years on the market.

Overall, I did manage to sufficiently clear bad energies so we could get Dave's radio station on the air. He says at regular interludes that if it wasn't for my help, the station wouldn't exist. Undoubtedly, from a distance, I cleared no less than seven demons and a hoard of entities from the house, yet it is one of those houses that just attract evil forces to it. Either way, if Dave and his family had stayed there, it would have destroyed them. One can ask if they will ever be free from that house. Personally, I don't know. I continue to dive in and try to free it from evil, but it's ongoing. After all, there are places on this planet that seem to have a permanent link to the dark. All begging the question as to whether an evil force leads them to this abode unwittingly, or whether it was simply bad luck? Anyway, *Paramania Radio* is growing and going from strength to strength. Truly, there have been times when Dave thought of pulling the plug, but since moving house, his radio station appears to have a bright future.

Chapter 7

Andy Porter—Psychic Surgeon

Anne and I got to know Andy Porter and his wife, Jayne, through a mutual friend some years ago. From time to time, we have helped each other to help others. Interestingly for us, Andy's spiritual journey began when he was living in Chippenham, Wiltshire, many years before we got to know him. Furthermore, he has talked about his psychic experiences from that period on my radio show many times.

Back then, Andy had no interest, or belief, in the supernatural. In fact, he ridiculed the notion of demons or ghosts. This was all to change, however, when he started to feel a presence in the room with him when he went to bed. Certainly, as the nights passed, things got scary—very scary. His bed (with Andy in it) would start to shake and then begin to levitate from the bedroom floor. This went on for quite a while until the point came when Andy decided that enough was enough; it was time to move home. It was around this time that he met with Jayne, who would later become his wife.

Unlike Andy, Jayne had an interest in the spiritual side of life. So, their coming together was not by chance; it was destined. As such, they were on an incredible journey together that would change their lives forever. All explaining why, following these bizarre experiences, Andy wanted to learn more about this other world he had discovered. Indeed, he listed spiritual groups in his locality and went to their meetings to get a better understanding of Spirit. Hence, it is no coincidence he was introduced to his spirit guide, 'Chen', at this time. However, little did Andy know what an important alliance they would make together! Andy started to have an interest in the human mind; in particular people who were diagnosed with Schizophrenia. This was something that Chen wanted Andy to pursue in order to help sufferers. Chen knew that not all people diagnosed as Schizophrenic were actually victims of this ailment. He knew some people with voices in their heads and split personalities were, in fact, possessed by demonic energies. Therefore, Chen taught Andy how to recognise these people. Thus, almost immediately, people started to come to him for help. By working alongside Chen, as well as linking in to these demons, Andy is able to remove bad energy, thereby allowing people to live a normal life.

Sometimes, of course, a client not only knows they are possessed, but also that bad energies are in their home. This is when Andy and I collaborate. In these cases, I will travel anywhere to clear people's homes. Between the two of us (with our spirit guides), we can make life better all round. Now let's get this in perspective! There are people who are Schizophrenic and have bad energies with them because illnesses attract negativity. Additionally, the removal of demons will not cure Schizophrenia. Hence, there is a fine line between being able to help or not. Yet, even if a person does have Schizophrenia, they are better off without demons possessing them. Stated so, Andy's work is ongoing and has proven invaluable in assisting people who seek his help.

With this work, as you can imagine, he comes into contact with demons regularly. Certainly, clients go to his home for treatment, which implies he was unfortunate in having to deal with some of these unwanted energies as they infested his own home. So similar to a dentist finding it impossible to pull their own teeth, Andy and Jayne asked Anne and I to go to their home to clear these unwanted presences—which we did. After the clearing, I explained to Andy and Jayne how to keep themselves and their home free from such infestations. Since then, Andy and I have been in regular contact with each other and, to this day, he has no bad energies there, even though he still has clients visit his home.

Andy is located in Wiltshire, England, but he is able to help people remotely—wherever in the world they live.

Chapter 8
A Few Significant Interviews

• **Christopher Saint Booth**

I had the pleasure and privilege to have interviewed some fascinating people on my radio show. For example, on the 12th December, 2012, through a connection with Jenny Stewart, the joint owner of *Paramania Radio*, I interviewed Christopher Saint Booth. Now, Chris and his brother Philip are at the top of their field as film producers. One of their many successes being the 2009 film *The Possessed*, based on a true account of the possession of a young girl named Lurancy Vennum. The film, like many of the Booth brothers' productions, enjoys a cult following (2).

In himself, Chris was a great guest. Moreover, he and his identical twin brother, Phil, were born in Halifax, Yorkshire, England. When they were seven years of age, the family immigrated to Canada. Curiously, Chris still has his English accent, with a touch of the 'transatlantic' in there. He explained in the interview that his first love was music and how he was greatly influenced by the Beatles. As such, he became lead singer with the pop group Sweeny Todd, taking over from Brian Adams. He even toured extensively with them.

Yet, Chris and Phil wanted to get into film making. Their interest was the occult and the paranormal. Critics have noted:

"Chris is a composer and producer, known for *Death Tunnel* (2005), *Spooked: The Ghosts of Waverly Hills Sanatorium* (2006) and *Children of the Grave* (2007)." Thus, it is hardly surprising he created *Spooked TV*, which is shown on *SYFY TV* Channel. Indeed, it became a huge success story.

• Daz Sampson

At the beginning of 2012, I was asked by John Sutton if I would like to have Daz Sampson as a guest on my show. By reputation, Daz is a pop star who, after a life-changing event that almost killed him, began his spiritual journey. As a man, Daz is a larger-than-life character, full of energy and vitality. So, Daz came on my radio show and has been back as my guest several times.

On each occasion, he has taken over, compelling me to joke (on air): "It is the Daz Sampson show, and I am his guest."

Overall, I cannot get a word in edgeways. This is because he is so enthusiastic about helping people that his passion overflows with every word he speaks—an enthusiasm giving him a loyal fan bases both musically and spiritually. Interestingly, Daz was born in Stockport, Cheshire, England, in 1974, going into radio broadcasting at the tender age of 17. He has even worked with Radio Luxembourg!

His heart, however, was in making music. In this regard, he has written many songs and remixed well-known songs like *Kung Foo Fighting,* which was a big hit for him. Furthermore, he represented the UK in the Eurovision Song Contest 2006, while having sung with several boy bands, including *Bus Stop, Rikki & Daz, Barn Dance Boys* and *United Nations*, not to mention singing solo. Therefore, it was a massive shift for him to leave this behind and follow his awakening.

Once he recalled on my show how, as a child, he saw a lady at school who told him he would be famous. He had gone out of class to use the toilet; no one was around. When walking down the corridor, however, he was stopped by this lady. At the time, Daz didn't realise she was dressed in clothes from a bygone era. Hence, he thought she was a teacher he hadn't seen before. The school, after all, was so big he thought nothing of it. Yet, over the next few years, he would get glimpses of her from time to time. Occasionally, she would be standing near the school railings or entrance—always alone. Indeed, Daz found out later that this lady had been a teacher at the school and had passed away some years before. Furthermore, throughout his life when things were hard, she would appear as if to reassure him all would be well. So, from his early years, Daz has always known he has a connection with Spirit, and he now uses it to help others. He is always upbeat and his positive.

New York Psychic Celebrity, JESSE BRAVO

A series of events led me to interviewing New York psychic celebrity Jesse Bravo. Jesse has been a guests on many TV chat shows and has appeared on *MTV*.

In the January of 2013, psychic medium, Wayne Isaacs was due to be my guest on *Understanding Spirit*. Just a few hours before the show Wayne called me to say he wouldn't be able to come on the show that night. Nonetheless, he wondered if promoter/writer John Sutton could be his replacement. Now, this change in guest turned out to be fate. This is because after getting to know John, who is the editor of *Psychic World Newspaper*, he wrote an article about me for the paper, while also introducing me to some very interesting and well-known people who are now my friends.

One of these people is Jesse Bravo. Curiously, from the moment we talked on the phone, we hit it off. I recorded the interview with him in March for the show to be aired in the May of 2013; this interview is still among my podcasts. Afterwards, we stayed in touch on a regular basis. This led to Jesse and I hosting a separate radio show together and proving Jesse to be a unique character; full of energy and charisma. Together, we created the show *Knowledge of Spirit* at www.knowlegeofspirit.com. Between the two of us, we bought great guests to the show. These included UK pop star turned psychic, Daz Sampson;, Michele Whitedove, voted America's number 1 psychic, John Holland; Carla Wills-Brandon; Lai Animal, communicator; British psychic medium, Tony Stockwell; the Witch Queen of New York, Lady Rhea; international British psychic medium, Angela McGhee; visionary, Dave Ashworth; internationally top psychic medium, Rev. Colin Fry; psychic medium, Derek Acorah; and Psychic surgeon, Andy Porter. Additionally, we interviewed psychic medium, Silvia Brown, which turned out to be the last interview she gave before, sadly, passing away in 2013. The one thing all these people have in common is the desire to help as many people they can and get the word out that our loved ones are safe and still with us in spirit.

We have a great friendship. Apart from doing future radio shows together, he is a regular contributor to the monthly online digital *Paranormal Galaxy Magazine*, wherein he writes articles.

Chapter 9
Scotland

Scotland is a country very special to Anne and I. From the very first time I crossed the English border, I felt its presence and my connection with this country and its people. This was a good many years before my 'Awakening'. In hindsight, my first visit there was through work and I was in wonderment at the scenery and atmosphere; it was as if I belonged there. Many years later, I took Anne with me so she could share the experience. I worked as a salesman in those days, selling dart equipment to pubs and social clubs. Thus, we both saw a great deal of Scotland. However, little did we both realise how significant this connection would be in our lives.

To start with, Anne found out a lot about herself whilst there, which accumulated during our many visits. Moreover, while driving from Dumbarton up to Inverness one time, we were passing the magnificent Loch Lomond and then Loch Ness, eventually coming to Urquhart Castle, which stands magnificently on the banks of Loch Ness. Anne said she had an overwhelming need to look round the castle. Now, the castle is run by Scotland's National Trust, even though it's mostly a ruin. Yet, parts are still standing and the views over the Loch are breath taking. Uncannily, on entering the grounds, Anne seemed transported into a bygone age. She became very emotional. Afterwards, we went into a small cinema to watch the re-enactment of the battles that took place at Urquhart Castle, along with a brief history of the people who lived there. Anne seemed to be filling in gaps to the history being recounted on film. When we came out of the cinema, Anne said that she could see herself all those hundreds of years ago and knew this had been her home. Then we walked through the grounds of the castle to the battlements overlooking Loch Ness, coming to a small walkway, where it became a dead end. The only way back into the main areas was by passing us. This needs saying, because sitting on a large rock close to a part of the remaining wall of the castle was a man dressed in a brown robe. His head bowed as if he was deep in thought.

Something prompted me to say to Anne, "That's your guide sitting there."

We then turned to each other, wondering if the man could be approached, before quickly turning back towards him. Unsurprisingly, he had vanished. Clearly, there was nowhere for him to have gone, because the pathway was too narrow for him to have passed us and the bank on the side away from the battlements was far too steep for anyone to climb. There was no one else around and the wind had stopped—producing an unnatural calmness at that moment. Suddenly, after a few seconds, the strong wind that had been blowing returned, and a group of eight people appeared. This special moment had passed, and all was back as it was before. Following this, Anne had words come into her head saying she will 'always be safe; I love you; I will protect you.'

From that time onwards, Anne has felt her guide with her all the time. Moreover, she has learned a lot about him; about their relationship in that bygone era. They were husband and wife; they fought, lived and loved together. Yet, he has never wanted to return to our dimension, although he has been with Anne (in spirit) throughout her lifetimes.

Anne is very protective of him; other than me, no one knows his identity.

Chapter 10
Highland Haunting

In the summer of 2010, I received a phone call from a lady named Shirley who needed help for her daughter who was being psychically attacked. Shirley, with her husband Frederick, had taken Natasha (their daughter) to see Andy Porter in order to find out if he could remove the demon(s) causing these attacks. Indeed, Andy had removed the entities. However, it was apparent there was a lot more to do in their home. Therefore, Andy told them to contact me, so Anne and I could visit their home in Scotland.

Now, their home wasn't an everyday run-of-the-mill house. In fact, it was a small 500-year-old hotel with four room lettings. As such, they had bought it five years previously. Looking back, Natasha was 14 at the time they bought the hotel. Yet, upon viewing the hotel with a mind to buying it, Natasha immediately said—even before entering the building—that she felt it was evil and her parents shouldn't buy it. Nevertheless, Shirley and Frederick had already enjoyed a successful career running hotels, restaurants, and bars all over the world. Furthermore, at the time of buying the hotel, they were running a restaurant in Central London. Hence, they remained deaf to Natasha's pleas.

Obviously, bad forces can make people believe that they are right and someone else is wrong. Such was the case here. Natasha, being only 14 at the time, had made her parents believe it was a child's way of expressing her wish of not wanting to move from where they were living in London. After all, she would have to leave behind her friends and move hundreds of miles away to a country she hadn't been to before—but they were wrong.

From the outside, the hotel appeared very ordinary. Certainly, it didn't look 500 years old. In itself, the building had many distinguishing features. It was just an unassuming construction. Standing almost in the middle of a quaint village, not far from the sea, its location seemed perfect. This was why Shirley and Frederick ignored Natasha's warnings and went ahead with the purchase.

As I have stated previously, I have travelled extensively throughout the British Isles because of work. There is hardly anywhere in the UK I haven't been. So, as Anne and I approached the hotel, I said to Anne that I had been in the hotel before, albeit many years previously. Indeed, when we went inside, I recognised the layout of the bar and restaurant, and although at the time of my previous visit I wasn't into the 'psychic thing', I remember feeling uneasy entering the building.

On this occasion, the journey up to Scotland had been horrendous. The M6 motorway, which can be difficult at the best of times, was particularly awful. We were caught in traffic jam after traffic jam. Our journey took nine hours when it should have taken six. Moreover, we had a number of close calls, narrowly avoiding crashes into other vehicles that seemed to appear from nowhere. Coincidentally, Shirley had phoned us a number of times, checking if we were all right. She knew our journey would be difficult; whenever anyone tried to help them, there were problems. Similar to visiting Andy Porter, their car broke down when they were almost at his home and they had to stay at the hotel they had booked whilst the car was fixed in a local garage. All meaning, they were too late for their appointment with Andy and had to rearrange it for the following day. This is typical; the demons continually try to stop someone getting the help they desperately need.

In the end, Anne and I arrived at around 6 pm. Shirley had closed the bar and restaurant for the day, so we could clear the hotel without the public knowing what was going on. There was only one occupied bedroom, and Shirley said their other guests wouldn't be back until late. Implying, of course, there was no time to lose. Thus, Anne and I started the clearing of the entire hotel straight away. Shockingly, the whole building was infested with entities (minor negative energies that can cling to us to drain our energies) that can make us unendingly tired and stop us from sleeping when we went to bed. They can also push us into frequently making wrong decisions, leading to problems in our lives. Henceforth, the clearing was taking a lot longer than usual. So, we stayed at their hotel that night in order for the clearing to continue the next morning when the guests had gone out for the day.

By 9 pm, Anne and I were very tired and hungry. Therefore, Frederick prepared a lovely meal for us and we joined him, Shirley, Natasha and Natasha's boyfriend, Lance, for the meal. Once at table, the conversation was very revealing. For her part, Natasha had fallen under bad influences and was taking drugs. Indeed, Lance was desperately trying to get her away from these so-called friends, but to no avail. Additionally, that night Natasha was going to stay at Lance's father's home; she had been doing this for nearly two weeks because her bedroom wasn't safe for her to sleep in. Horrifyingly, she had been constantly (psychically) attacked whilst trying to sleep in that room.

Predictably, this room was the first on our agenda for clearing the next day. I knew that I would need to have all my energy and wits about me for this one. Especially, since Natasha had seen the Devil himself appear in her bedroom on several occasions, as well as his assisting demons. Interestingly, these demons appeared as transparent, small creatures about two feet high. Their eyes were red, their feet were long with talons not toes, while their arm and leg joints were the opposite way round to ours; like a flamingo's. Unsurprisingly, Natasha and Lance planned to return early the next morning to witness the clearing of her room.

I have to say at this point, Natasha's link with Spirit is phenomenal. She sees everything around her and connects with angels and spirits readily. Clearly, she understood why she had been led into temptation with drink and drugs. In herself, she wanted to end these addictions. However, every time she had walked away from the friends who encouraged her in these habits, she felt an energy pulling her back to them.

But, I digress. Natasha said she would instantly know when the bedroom was clear—and she did. I stood at the foot of the bed and saw in my third eye six demons, one in each corner of the room. I saw one over the bed behind me and one right in front of me—only a foot away. Meanwhile, my guide Ronaldo, as well as Anne's guide, were beside us with ten other trusted guides. The attack and subsequent battle was furious. It seemingly lasted an eternity but, in fact, was around two minutes. One by one (through my energy and the guides' power), these negative forces were dispatched to the glorious white light. I could see it through my third eye. This would be a one-way trip for these particular demons. Finally the devil had gone. At the end of the day, he is a coward and soon departs when he is going to be defeated.

All became calm, although I knew everything wasn't clear. Indeed, just as I was going to say what I was seeing, Natasha also saw what I was seeing. She said that there was a link, a portal, in the hotel from the underworld. If it wasn't closed up, more demons would come through. Certainly, this hotel was like a boat with a hole in its hull. It kept filling up as it was being emptied. So, I stood there and, with my guide's help, closed the portal.

Now, the hotel with its well-appointed location should have been full all year round. However, during the time this family had been there, the occupancy had fallen to a point of financial drowning. Even local people were not frequenting the hotel for meals or a drink. Now, I understand this could have been due to people not liking the owners, service, or décor. Following our meeting with the family, however, one could tell they were warm friendly people who had already run a successful hotel and catering concern, which had taken them to many countries around the world, including Saudi Arabia, Spain and Qatar. Hence, this decline in business was not down to them. Furthermore, they discovered this hotel had boasted of many previous owners who left after a couple of years; maybe they too had witnessed strange goings on.

Anyway, after the clearing, Natasha was on the way to recovery. Her drug problem ended just as quickly as it had begun. Also, she had no withdrawal symptoms. She didn't even go for counselling or get on a drug rehabilitation programme. Her craving just stopped. This shows evil forces had her in their grip. Once they had been removed, she was again in control of her own life. Indeed, she distanced herself from her 'druggy' friends and life was good. That is until several months down the line, when Natasha and her boyfriend decided to rent a house together.

It was then they moved into what seemed to be a lovely two-bedroomed, semi-detached house on a private housing estate about ten miles away from her parents' hotel. Overall, Natasha and Lance had been living there for around two weeks when demonic forces were at work again on Natasha, and this time Lance as well. Again, Anne and I were called upon to go up to clear this house for them, albeit staying as guests of Frederick and Shirley. Obviously, the hotel was fine; no further problems reported. The following day we went to Natasha and Lance's house to see what was going on. Now this is when it gets complicated. I soon realised that it was Natasha that the devil was targeting, not the family. The devil had led Natasha to a house that already had paranormal activity. They found out too late that the previous tenants had left as soon as the tenancy agreement was up for renewal.

Undoubtedly, this house was a different kind of challenge to the hotel. The demons were manifesting themselves. Natasha and Lance were seeing them in the form of demons, odd people and weird children. Indeed, strange energies would appear as wavy-coloured patterns on the walls of the lounge, as well as their bedroom. On separate occasions, Natasha and Lance had been pushed down the stairs. Lance had even sprained his right ankle and Natasha her left wrist. It was like a war zone. Hence, Anne and I went around the house with Natasha and Lance to locate the demons and remove them. Quite amazingly, Natasha showed no fear at all; she was just angry that these events were having such an impact on her life. Lance, on the other hand, was really nervous.

The clearing took about three hours to complete. Moreover, I saw a direct link to a demon lair that was targeting Natasha. Well, you might ask why they were targeting her? Let me stress again: her link to good spirits was phenomenal. For someone of such a young age, she understood the fight between good and evil, proved by the fact that she was always there to help others at the expense of herself while these things were happening. So, once the entire house was clear, I was able to clear all the links from the demons to Natasha and Lance. Everything was done and normality restored.

Overall, peace was restored at the hotel and Natasha's home, but the damage done had left its mark on the business. The decline in revenue had been going on for a long time before the family had asked me for help. Indeed, it had become so bad they were struggling to keep their financial heads above water. Thus, in 2013, they decided to sell up and move to England. Sadly, Natasha's relationship also ended at this time. Following this, she met a man called Simon, and all of them moved down together. In the case of Frederick and Shirley, they now run a pub/restaurant, whilst Natasha works with them. What is more, Simon and Natasha moved into a house of their own and have a beautiful baby girl named Lucy. All in all, they finally left the entire trauma behind them.

Chapter 11
Milton Keynes

In 2007, I received a phone call from Douglas Bedford—who lives in Milton Keynes with his wife, Amy, and his eight children. He asked if I would visit him, so that he and his future wife could have healing. He explained they had both been involved in a horrific car accident. An incident wherein they had just pulled into a petrol station (Douglas was just about to get out of their car to fill it up with fuel) when a car with blacked-out windows hurtled on to the forecourt at about 70 miles per hour. Out of control, this car lifted into the air, clearing the pumps and landed on its roof. Astoundingly, the driver freed himself from the wreckage and fled the scene (3). However, Douglas and Amy were trapped in their car and had to be freed by the fire brigade. Each had severe injuries to their legs, whilst Douglas had further injuries to his head. Fortunately, none of their children were with them at the time, being cared for by grandparents. Therefore, after a long stay in hospital, they were discharged with an array of painkillers to aid their recovery. For their parts, both Douglas and Amy had metal plates inserted in their legs.

Up to this point, Douglas had no interest, or belief, in the psychic and spiritual worlds. However, one evening, he and Amy were watching TV when a programme came on about alterative healing. After watching it, they thought that the conventional way of recovery didn't seem to be working, or at least was taking a long time. Moreover, their pains were becoming unbearable day after day, nagging away at both of them. An additional problem being that Douglas ran a successful small business, employing two people who relied on him for their income. So, they decided they would go online and find a healer. Out of the many healers/psychics that are on the web, Douglas was drawn to me.

Once connected, Anne and I drove 80 miles to see them. On entering their home, I could feel the intense, heavy atmosphere. I recall saying to Douglas that before I gave them healing, I would need to clear their home of the negative energies in there. He looked at me in bemusement, not understanding what I meant.

Anyway, he said, "Okay, go ahead."

At this juncture, I asked them to come with us around their house, so they could see what we were doing and feel the positive difference in the atmosphere. Douglas told me later when we were going around their home, he almost wanted to tell us to leave, thinking we were mad after witnessing what we were doing. Yet, he didn't. All meaning, two hours later, the clearing was done. I then told him I could now begin the hands-on healing. Douglas replied he felt he was getting addicted to the painkillers, while also taking other over the counter pills to try and cope with the pain. In the background, their hospital and family doctor said the operations had been a success, but their recovery would take a long time because of the severity of their injuries.

Anyway, I gave healing to Douglas, first on his legs, then his head. Afterwards, I gave healing to Amy. When I had finished them both, they exclaimed their pain had gone. Each of them was amazed, even though they had watched a show that filmed people having great results from healing.

Following this, Douglas asked if I would give healing to his seven-year-old son, in the hope it would help him with his behavioural problems. He had become a very disruptive little boy, terrorising their neighbourhood by fighting with other children in the street, breaking windows and generally running amok. Tellingly, his other children were not like this. Moreover, the lad was on the verge of being excluded from school. All meaning, for a long period, Douglas had been called regularly into the school about his son's activities. So, Douglas told his son to sit next to me and not move, which, amazingly, he did. Afterwards, I put my hands on the lad's head and kept them there for about 10 minutes. I could feel a lot of movement coming through my hands into him. When I had finished, Douglas asked me to heal all of his children, which I also did.

Just before Anne and I were leaving, Douglas said he had five vehicles at the front of the house that belonged to him; two work vans and three cars. He was having problems with one van. It wouldn't start first time and there were noises coming from the engine and gearbox. He had taken it to the garage where he always had his repairs and servicing done, but they were mystified with the problems because they couldn't find what was wrong. Therefore, I went outside and put my dowser's pendulum over the front bonnet and linked in with my spirit guides. I cleared the demon and six entities that were there. The next time Douglas started the van, there was a tremendously loud bang, although it ran perfectly. Indeed, other than having it serviced a few months later, he has had no problems with it since then. All our work was now complete, so Anne and I made our way back home. After a clearing, Anne and I always thank our guides for their help. After all, it is a partnership. My guides tell me they need my connection and energy to come into our dimension, while I need their energy to connect with the spirit world so this work can be done. Equally, we thank God for giving us the ability to be able to help people.

Early on the following Monday evening, I received a phone call from Douglas.

His opening words were, "What have you done to my son?"

I said, somewhat shocked, "What do you mean?"

I was worried, in case something was amiss. Replying, Douglas said there was a total transformation in his son's behaviour. For the rest of the weekend, his son had not been cheeky and had not terrorised any children. In fact, he had been kind to them and played happily with whomever he was with. Additionally, the day Douglas went to meet his son from school, the head teacher saw Douglas waiting to collect him and said the teachers couldn't understand the transformation in his son, asking what had created such a positive change. Douglas told them, whilst she looked at him lost for words. Overall, his son's behaviour has stayed good. However, he is a boy and has his moments, even though nothing like before.

When all said and done, Douglas is a remarkable man. Through challenging private circumstances, he won custody of seven of his children over his ex-wife. Furthermore, he supports his other son who lives with his ex-girlfriend, whilst that child spends time with his half brothers and sisters. Indeed, Amy and Douglas got married. Happily, Anne and I were invited to the ceremony. For her part, Amy took in all of Douglas's children, and now they have a daughter of their own. Since that time, Douglas has had me help his mother, father, and many other family members, as well as neighbours. He has additionally been a guest on my radio show, and when I was interviewed on local BBC Radio, he phoned in to tell his story. We keep in touch, and I recently mentioned to him I was writing a book about my experiences.

When asked if I could tell his story, he answered, "If it helps you to help others, then please do. You and Anne have changed my life completely, for the better."

My response was, "It is good to have you and your family as friends."

Chapter 12
Vikings

Back in 2004, I gave readings at a Mind, Body and Spirit Fayre held in the city of Hereford, England. In order to tell this story, I have changed the names of the people involved to respect their privacy.

A lady named Fran came to me and asked for a reading. It was apparent that this was not going to be a run-of-the-mill 'fortune telling' type of reading. Indeed, having sat down at my table, she said she had been drawn to me, believing I would be the person who could help her. Afterwards, she asked if I could tell her about her husband, Richard. Immediately, I told her that his behaviour over the past three weeks had unexplainably altered. He had become very agitated towards her and their two children and was totally out of character. Moreover, he had become violent towards Fran, although he hadn't raised his hand on the children. Nonetheless, his temper was greatly upsetting them. I added that there was some connection between him and Vikings. Fran said everything I had told her was exactly how things were and proceeded to ask how I could help her family. I said I would need to come to their home to clear the demons around them. This was arranged at a time when her partner (Richard) would be at work, five days later. She said she felt she couldn't tell him about me going there to clear everything, in case he refused the help.

When I arrived at their home, I could feel bad energies from outside the property. The house was a listed building dating back to Elizabethan times. It was a black and white timber-framed building, typical of that era, situated in the countryside, just outside a village. Obviously, I asked Fran to come around her home with me. I always do this so the client can witness the cleansing and feel the difference in the atmosphere straight away. Now, there were three demons in the house, two in the lounge and one in Fran and Richard's bedroom. Also, I could see the link to Richard from the six Viking warriors possessing him. Fran said Richard was buying as many books as he could about Vikings and hiring them out from the library, whilst simultaneously watching innumerable videos about them. His obsession had gone to ridiculous lengths. So, I linked in, with my spirit guides, to Richard, using Fran as the connection and, one by one, removed these Vikings away from him.

The following evening I received a phone call from Fran. She had told Richard all about the events of the day before. Evidently, when he returned home from work, he had reverted to his loving and caring self. He said, at about 3 pm that afternoon, he had felt something lift from him and he suddenly felt light and free of dark thoughts. Furthermore, he started to reflect within himself why he had been obsessed with Vikings. As such, there was no reason he could think of as to why this had happened. After all, they lived nowhere near the sea and the Vikings had invaded Great Britain by landing on the coasts of Scotland, as well as the North East of England. Tellingly, Herefordshire is situated in the South West of England and along the borders of Wales. Hence, there was no obvious connection. Overall, I never found out the connection, even though I believe it could have been a previous life for Richard. When Richard came on the phone, I wondered what he would say to me. However, I needn't have worried. He said he was grateful for what I had done and wanted to meet me in person. Thus, we arranged a get together for the following Saturday. Anne hadn't accompanied me on the clearing, but came with me to meet him and Fran.

Looking back, it was a lovely, sunny, warm Saturday summer's day when we went to visit them. What is more, Richard was welcoming to us both. We also met their son and daughter, who were lovely children, aged about 10 and 8. We sat in the beautiful back garden; the flowers were in full bloom, the smell of the hyacinths wafted across to us from the borders—the setting was perfect. Thereafter, Richard asked me to explain fully what had gone on the day of the clearing. I explained there were a number of bad spirits in their home.

Curiously, some seem to have been inherited with the house, albeit accompanied by a strong presence of Viking soldiers. He said that about four months previously, he had been watching a television documentary about the Viking invasion of Britain and had now come to realise this was when his obsession began. Additionally, he said to me he could see himself as one of them—it all seemed so real to him. I said even though I can't categorically say he had been a Viking in a previous life, it did seem the most obvious reason for his personality change. For his part, Richard said he had hated himself for the way he had behaved towards his family. He could see it happening as if watching a movie, wherein he was a character in the film. He said he had no control over his actions and this really scared him. Fran retorted that Richard was now back to being the loving husband and father he had always been.

Tangentially, Richard said he had been having severe stomach pains periodically over the last few months and asked if I would give him hands-on healing. As such, we withdrew to the house and I proceeded to put my hands upon his stomach. Straight away, I could feel a pulling in my hands, whereas Richard thought my hands were inside him. That's how strong the healing energy was right then. Now, this went on for around ten minutes or so. I then withdrew my hands from Richard's stomach. Overall, it's hard to explain, but when the healing is finished, my hands are released from the person's being. Until that moment, however, it is as if they are glued in their position, and I can't let go. Clearly, this is when the doctor in spirit (Dr Ingles who works through me) is doing his work to help my client. Unsurprisingly, at the moment of release, Richard said all his pain had left him. He said it was as if it had been drawn out of his body. All was now well.

We continued to have a lovely afternoon in the garden, sipping typical English tea with sandwiches and cakes. A month later, I heard from Fran saying the whole family were really happy and their lives were back on track.

Chapter 13
Voodoo

Some years ago, a young lady phoned me asking for help. She had been looking for someone who could help her and had called into a spiritual centre in her hometown to ask if they could assist. Yet the person there said this wasn't the type of work they did, but knew someone who could probably be approached—that person was me. Now the lady's parents had both died and, as an only child, she had inherited their home in Jamaica. Simultaneously, relatives over there were trying to sell the house for themselves, even though they had no legal right to do so. Fortunately, another relative of hers realised what was going on and stopped it happening in time.

Unexplained things started happening to her. Her relationship ended for no reason. Her partner said it was over and just left. Moreover, as a singer and songwriter, her bookings suddenly dried up at the same time as she started having problems with her health. Indeed, her top lip swelled to the point where she found it difficult to talk, never mind sing. Thereafter, one of her legs and feet became so painful, she could hardly walk. What is more; she visited her doctor, who couldn't find the causes to these problems. Hence, he referred her to the local hospital, wherein a consultant couldn't explain the problems either. Tests were done, but to no avail. It was a mystery to each of them. Eventually, Anne and I went to her home in Greater Manchester to see if we could help. I will call her Naomi, since she has asked for her identity to be protected for obvious reasons.

It goes without saying, the moment I entered Naomi's home, I could feel the heavy, repressive presence of many bad energies. She said her own energy had also been depleted and she had no 'get-up-and-go'. Furthermore, the subsequent work problems had been going on for about four months.

Meanwhile, Naomi had tried to get other types of employment (shop or factory work), but without any success. Indeed, there was even the possibility of her own home being repossessed. At this juncture, she showed us photos of the Jamaican house she was trying to sell, and there seemed no reason for it not being purchased. Indeed, the house overlooked the sea and stood in its own grounds. All meaning, it was only through the watchful eye of her cousin that this criminal sale was stopped. Amazingly, no successful prosecution happened to the perpetrators involved in the attempted fraud.

Anyway, Anne and I found no less than nine demons in Naomi's house—four working on her from Jamaica. I cleared the house and then set on removing the demons in Jamaica. This was no easy feat; not only did I have to clear the bad from there, but equally make sure nothing would manifest with her again. Additionally, there was the issue of keeping Anne and myself psychically safe from these people in Jamaica. In this respect, I called upon God, Jesus and Sai Baba, as well as my guides, to help and protect all of us in the house. Nevertheless, the whole process took nearly five hours. Indeed, throughout the clearing, as soon as an entity was removed, I could feel others attacking me. Usually, of course, when performing a clearing, other bad energies will back off and try to hide. Not these ones, however. This time, it was out-and-out war between me and them. Twice during this clearing, I felt demons trying to enter my body space. Yet, on both occasions my spirit guides stopped them. Unsurprisingly, the moment the house was clear of all these energies, the atmosphere changed for the better. Each room became lighter; the oppressive feeling had gone. Furthermore, the swelling in Naomi's lip had disappeared, after which she said the pains in her leg and foot had also gone. Now, whether Naomi's ethnic background gave her a belief in such curses, or it was real, isn't the point. Rather, it is the reality of suffering that counts. The fact is, with everything clear, she is able to get on with her life again.

It is a terrible truth that some people are jealous of others and either want what doesn't rightfully belong to them, or want the downfall of another person. Two months after the clearing, however, Naomi found a buyer for the house in

Jamaica—which was duly sold. Moreover, she has cut all her real and emotional ties with Jamaica. She says although she had visited there quite a few times when she was growing up and had been on holiday there with her ex-partner, it wasn't somewhere she ever wanted to go any more. Said so, she was born in England.

"I am British and my life is in Britain. All of my friends and loved ones are here; I know who I am now," she stated.

It goes without saying that the music industry is a hard profession to be in, but now Naomi is in the process of making an album. What is more; she has been successful in getting a job, so she can pay the arrears off on her mortgage and live properly again. All in all, the whole experience lasted nearly eight years before she contacted me, which is why this account can't relay the real emotional and physical effect it had on her. However, each day she says she is getting stronger. Clearly, good will always overcomes the bad energies, but it can be a struggle. Thus, the answer is not to give in, since justice will prevail in the end.

Chapter 14
Bodmin Moor

In June of 2009, Anne and I booked two stands to do readings and sell our crystals and crystal jewellery at the Fairy Fest in Cornwall. It was a three-day event; Friday through to the Sunday, which was held at Collingford Lake Park on Bodmin Moor. Now, to this day, Bodmin Moor is a lonely foreboding place. Once you leave the main A30 trunk road that dissects it, visitors quickly discover the setting for Daphne Du Maurer's famous novel Jamaica Inn. Indeed, the actual inn still exists to this day. As an aside, I should mention that the festival was being held on the same weekend as the world famous Glastonbury Festival.

The Fairy Fest, of course, is a celebration of all things spiritual and mystical. All meaning, there were some good musical bands and singers providing the entertainment, even though the majority of people attending were dressed as fairies. Can I just add here that Anne and I didn't dress as fairies, nothing wrong with the people who did, but it just wasn't our thing.

Stated so, most people camped on site, although Anne and I had booked into a hotel in the town of Bodmin, which lies about 10 miles south of the Moor. Hence, on the second day (Saturday morning), we were travelling to the festival around 9.30 am. Usually, the A30 is a fast road with no central barrier between oncoming traffic on the part that leads to the Moor. Anne and I, therefore, were travelling at about 60 miles per hour down quite a steep hill whereon little traffic was present. Indeed, nothing was following us, apart from a few cars in the near distance. For my part, I was driving and could see we were approaching a crossroads where we had right of way. Opposite, there was a small car waiting to cross over to a nearby country lane. Without warning, the driver pulled out in front of us. What happened next was incredible. The control of my steering wheel was wrested from me, and the car was steered to the wrong side of the road. At the same time, it seemed as if the oncoming traffic was frozen in time, while the car coming out of the side lane hit the passenger rear door of our car. All pushing us further over. Then the two cars were released from each other, and we found ourselves (along with the other car) back on the correct side of the road, albeit parked on a verge. Afterwards, all the other cars went past us as if nothing had happened, whereas I got out of my car and walked towards the offending vehicle.

Simultaneously getting out of her car, the young lady driver was visibly shaken.

She kept saying, "I am sorry, I am sorry."

This made me retort, "Are you alright?"

Fortunately, she was. There didn't seem to be any physical injuries. I assured her this was the main thing; everything else could be sorted-out later.

After all, "It's only metal. Let's have a look what the damage is done," I said.

At this point, I looked at the front of her car. Back then, it didn't fully register with me that there appeared no dents. So, we walked to the side of my car where the impact had happened. Astonishingly, there was no damage at all to our car, making us both stare with incomprehension. By this time, I had asked for her name, which was 'Rachael'.

Nevertheless, she looked at me and kept repeating. "But I hit you, I hit you, I hit you hard!"

Immediately, Rachael insisted on giving me her home address and phone number, in case I found a problem with the car later. She said she was 21 years of age and hadn't long passed her driving test. Furthermore, she lived with her parents on a farm just up the country lane she was crossing towards. Thereafter, I gave her one of my business cards, which freaked her out, because the card clearly says I am a psychic investigator.

Perhaps, this made me add, "We were obviously being looked after by a higher force."

Obviously, we all went our way trying to make sense of what had just happened. Meaning, when we arrived at the

Fairy Fest; neither I, nor Anne, could contain these events to ourselves, and we told our fellow exhibiting neighbours about the accident. Word spread and lots of people came to us to hear the story first-hand. One could say we became the talk of the festival.

The following day, I decided to phone to see if Rachael was all right. Her father answered the phone.

He said, "Oh, you are the kind gentleman who was so nice and understanding to Rachael yesterday."

Following this, he added he had never known his daughters tell a lie. Hence, as incredible as the story was, and with me phoning, he totally accepted the account of events. Interestingly, he stated he had closely examined Rachael's car, and the only damage he had found was that the two front headlights had been pushed slightly back, after which he corrected them for her. Now, that in itself was a miracle, because the headlamps on that model of car are set slightly back from the front bumper and couldn't be struck without breaking the bumper.

Her father also said if we were ever their way at any time, we should call in for a cup of tea and lunch. We haven't taken up that kind offer yet, since it is a remote part of the country and it's somewhere we only occasionally visit. Nonetheless, I did have an email from Rachael a year later—almost to the exact day of the accident—saying she will always remember that extraordinary day and thanking me again for my kindness.

God and spirit work in incredible ways. We were all truly looked after that day.

Chapter 15
On Culloden Moor

Fascinatingly, in 2009, Anne and I went on holiday to Scotland, which as I said previously is our spiritual home. So, having travelled extensively over the years to all parts of the country, we found ourselves in Inverness—the gateway to the Highlands. It's truly a magical part of the world, where the North Sea meets the mountains and lochs, including the famous Loch Ness. Overall, we had visited this area many times before, but this time was unforgettable, while the series of psychic events were incredible.

Looking back, it was in early June of that year when Anne and I found ourselves on Culloden Moor. It was about 8.30 in the evening and we were driving away from Inverness to where we were staying. As such, I saw a road sign pointing to the Moor. Now, at that time of year in Northern Scotland, it stays light until the early hours of the morning. Indeed, even then there is some light in the sky. Hence, I said to Anne I had an overwhelming need to go on the Moor, whereon we pulled on to the car park of the visitor centre. Once there, we saw a motor home, car and a motorbike parked, whilst the centre building itself was closed for the night. Nonetheless, there was open access to the Moor, so we left the car and walked along a pathway that led to it.

Walking towards us were two people in motorcycle gear, who said, "Hello," and left the Moor.

Then two couples passed us as they too went back to their vehicles. Thereafter, we found ourselves alone. However, a short way along the well-trodden path, we came to a lectern that provided information about the Battle of Culloden in 1746. Now, the lectern was positioned so that whilst reading, one could look over at the main area where the fighting occurred. Indeed, this battle was a particularly bloody affair, wherein the Scots fought the English to keep hold of their own country; a battle they lost. Sadly, there was a terrible loss of many lives on each side. Unexpectedly, as Anne and I moved away from the lectern, I was confronted (in spirit) by 83 Scottish soldiers asking to be moved on from the battleground. To facilitate this, I stood there holding my pendulum-dowser in my hand; I have it with me always. Thus, I linked in with them and sent them to the light; I felt their gratitude. Overall, it was an overpowering feeling of warmth that showed they were free from a long-lasting nightmare.

Following this, we continued our walk along the designated pathways. We turned right, and then continued ahead to the next right turn. The Moore had been divided into separate areas with paths going off in all directions. Moreover, there are low ranch-style fences separating the battlefields. We read this had been done to keep control of the bracken that grew there and a flock of Marino sheep were used to prevent this bracken from taking over the fields. As such, they were moved from area to area as and when necessary.

At this juncture, Anne was looking at the sheep in the area to our left, although my attention had been directed over to the lectern we had stood by on entering the Moore. Please note, each of these sectioned off areas was about as long and wide as a football field. In which case, I was looking across the width of a wide field. Suddenly, I saw a brown round object with a yellow centre that looked as if it was balancing on top of the lectern. I stared at it, then it started moving from left to right and back again across the top of the lectern, getting quicker with every rotation.

Finally, I said to Anne, "Look at this, what's going on?"

Thereafter, we both stood riveted to the spot, trying to make out what was happening. Curiously, at this point the object stopped and began to rise slowly. It then became clear. The object was a Tammy Shanty; a kind of flat round hat/cap worn by Scotsmen. Thence, the head beneath it came into view. A very angry energy omitted from this person. Anne and I both felt it even from the distance that was between him and us. Nevertheless, I could make out a thick, long grey beard. His gaze seemed fixed on each of us as he moved to his right at the side of the lectern. I recall him being a well-built, tall, big man. He was dressed in full Scottish battledress; kilt and tunic, even though his feet seemed to be wrapped around with rags. From the distance we were apart, I was grateful of the space between us. Anyway, footwear aside, he stamped his feet in rage before turning away from us and eventually disappearing behind some trees. Anne and I looked at each other, not knowing what to make of this occurrence.

Then, in spirit, I saw the battle being played-out in front of us. Anne, however, didn't see it. Shockingly, there were hundreds of soldiers fighting and being killed, or injured. It was as if I was there with them observing every bloody detail. This seemed to last for an eternity, but in reality for less than a minute. Afterwards, the image of this man came into my third eye. He said he was John Macgregor and I had no right to remove his soldiers. What is more, he added I had not seen the last of him. In the material world, however, we eventually started to make our way back to the car, while I said to Anne we needed to walk past that lectern to get back to our car. Obviously, neither of us looked forward to it. Yet, he had gone, whilst all of this had taken place in less than an hour. Thereafter, we got back into the car and made our way back to the hotel.

Now, I have done some research into 1746 and the McGregor's. Sadly, there is no account of individual people from the Clan McGregor. Nonetheless, the Clan was persecuted over a long period of time, and historians do say some McGregor's did fight at Culloden. Bear in mind, that stated, I am just relating my experiences and not writing a historical account.

The following day, we had decided to make the 100 mile journey to John O'Groats; the most northerly point of the UK's mainland. Overall, the day went well, and we enjoyed a lovely time taking in the scenery and the wildness of the North Sea. Eventually, of course, we started our journey back to the hotel, but by a different route—inland. So, it became apparent how high up we were when looking over to the west and realising only the peaks of the Highland mountains were visible. Regardless, the road we were on was quiet flat with fields spanning out to our right and trees to our left. Moreover, this road was classed as a main road, even though there didn't seem to be much traffic. Anyway, I spied in the distance (perhaps half a mile away) an articulated lorry travelling towards us. It was going round an acute bend in the road, while on either side of the road there were deep ditches with no protective barriers in place. As the lorry began to come out of the bend, a black car with blackened-out windows came straight towards us on the wrong side of the road—at speed.

I braked frantically, saying to Anne, "This is it. We are gone."

Yet, steering as close to the edge of the road as I could, I saw the lorry was also braking. Somehow, the blackened-out car missed the front of the lorry and the front of our car with just inches to spare. It was, I would still say to this day, the scariest moment I have lived through. Indeed, I was shaking. Equally, Anne was shaking. I found a place to stop—at which point, the image of John McGregor came into my third eye to tell me he was trying to kill us. Strangely, the car and lorry had gone. However, I felt a divine presence with us at that moment. We had been saved! The rest of the journey was spent in quiet reflection on what could have been. Be under no doubt there are deep, dark forces out there. We have to be mindful of our actions, since actions have consequences as I learned that day.

Chapter 16
How to Help

Like so many people, I set out to help others and, by using my connection with Spirit, I have been able to do this. There are times though when an individual can't be helped. This happens when they are in denial of their real deep-seated emotional problems. It is an issue, therefore, which is probably karmic. Furthermore, it is possible for a person to ask for assistance, but their subconscious mind isn't ready to release them, so they can move on.

An example of this is found some years ago, when I was approached by a young lady, who at the time was in her thirties. She had had a bad experience as a young teenager; almost losing her life because of a gas leak in her home. Sadly, this affected her mind. All meaning, entities and demons entered her to create a living hell within her. Moreover, by the time she found me through my website, she had already been seeking help from quite a few other psychics and healers. Indeed, she even went to Australia to find someone who could release her from the voices in her head and the images she saw in her third eye. Needless to say, her torment led her to try and take her own life, on at least two occasions.

Now, at her family home, there was an orchard wherein she twice put a rope around her neck and jumped. Fascinatingly, even though there was no cry for help, God must have been watching over her. After all, on both occasions, she was her father. Obviously, following this, her family had all the overhanging (gallows) branches cut off.

Eventually finding myself on the case, I flew over to Ireland on four occasions to help her by clearing these bad energies away—from the house, surrounding lands, and herself. Now, once a clearing is done, it is usual that no more bad energies infest someone again, since this person is ready to move on and psychically protect themselves. This time, however, the recipient had become paranoid and believed all the people she had sought help from were linking into her mind and tormenting her. Nonetheless, she lived a full life travelling across the world, horse riding and so on; she even had her own car. When I reached there, she had a magazine about horses rested on the steering wheel. During the hour-long journey to her family home, she continued to read it. She said she had to keep looking at the pictures, otherwise the demons would get into her mind and body. I tried to tell her this wasn't the case, yet she wouldn't listen to me. Therefore, it was a nerve-racking, terrifying journey. Thankfully, most of it was in the countryside. Even though before we left the towns, there were a few close calls. Indeed, she was oblivious to cars parked at the roadside, and I needed to tell her to look where we were heading or we would crash into the back of them.

On my last visit, her mother drove me back to the airport. I explained I had done all I could to help her daughter over a period of time I had known her. I explained that, on many occasions, I had told her daughter she needed professional psychiatric help. The mother said they too had tried, but she wouldn't take any medication prescribed. In which case, her father and mother were at their wits' end about the ongoing situation. Additionally, their daughter had run up debts due to phone readings from psychics all over the world amounting to over eighty thousand pounds. So, her parents paid her credit cards off in the hope their daughter would start afresh with her life. Unfortunately, this obviously wouldn't be the case.

Unsurprisingly, the young lady became obsessed with me, believing I was the only one who understood her and could keep the demons at bay. Yet, I told her I could do no more to help. All in all, things were becoming unhealthy in that she wanted to hear from me on a daily basis—albeit, if I said there were no bad energies with her, she then stated I was wrong. They were there, but hiding, she would insist. At one time, a month passed in silence, although this proved to be the calm before the storm. Thence one morning, at 8.30am, there was a banging on our front door, and she stood demanding that Anne and I help her. She had caught an early flight across and hired a car to get to us. Moreover, she had blocked our driveway with her car so that we couldn't leave. I told her to come back in a couple of hours since we had things to do. When she had left, I immediately called her mother, who in turn phoned her daughter to persuade her to go back home on the next available flight. Yet, the girl wouldn't leave until I had talked to her, which I did later in the day. Clearly, it was very unsettling to see someone going through the anguish she was going through. Thus, I consoled her and got her to see she needed to return home. Nowadays, the young lady had been prescribed medication by her doctor and hospital. Nevertheless, she won't take them because she believes they cannot help her. As such, she is in a vicious circle, desperately seeking help, yet not taking the right kind of help.

I knew some so-called psychics in the past had taken lots of money from her while doing nothing for her. For my part, I had long stopped asking for money from her. She would often send me a cheque through the post, but I would return it due to the fact I knew there was nothing psychical to be removed. Also, I am not in the business of taking financial advantage of clients. Meaning, after this incident, I had numerous answer phone messages from her. Following which, I called her father and told him. Thereafter, these messages stopped for about a year, although they then started up again. Once more, I contacted her father, and they stopped. Currently, a couple of years on, I have heard no more from her. All I can say is that I sincerely hope she has accepted professional help. However, I doubt it.

Once the bad energies are removed from someone and their situation doesn't alter, there is nothing an honest psychic can do to help. Indeed, there occasionally is a fine line between removing bad energies and a person believing they are continually under attack. When all said and done, the mind is very complicated. We don't understand it fully. So, once a responsible psychic has done their work, they need to convey to the client that other professional help has to be sought. The problem is that some clients are likely to go and consult other psychics, since they believe the spiritual problem remains with them. Afterwards, if that other psychic is of a mind to take financial advantage of this person, they tell them there is still a problem—and on it goes.

Obviously, the vast majority of psychics are good, honourable people who want to help their clients. However, there are a few bad apples spoiling things, thereby tarring others with the same brush.

Chapter 17
A Life-Changing Friendship

I had the privilege to know the late Manny Fox as a close, personal friend, a Broadway producer, no less. Now, how I came to know and love this extraordinary man, I will outline here below. Yet, to fully set the scene, we have to go back to 2005, as well as a series of remarkable events leading to this bond.

As I previously related, it was in the November of that year when a documentary on Channel 4 (4) aroused my attention. Indeed, as Anne and I watched, it became clear that this programme had been made by conspiracy theorists David Icke and his then wife, Pamela (5). Obviously, we didn't stay in touch with David, even though we did with Pamela. A significant choice directly connected to my eventual meeting with Manny. It was more than synchronicity, after all, Pamela was originally from Phoenix and nowadays lives in Sedona, Arizona. Hence, by November 2010, Pamela found herself at the checkout of an organic food store in Sedona, paying for her groceries when Manny came along and in typical (Manny) fashion joined in the conversation that Pamela was having with the cashier. Obviously, Manny and Pamela didn't know each other. However, there was a café in the store, and they went and had coffee together. Spontaneously, Manny told Pamela all his problems including how, at the age of 75, he was going through a nasty divorce from his wife, Cinda Firestone Fox. He also told her that Cinda had taken everything from him and he was living on spousal support. Pamela said she knew someone who could help him spiritually and gave him my email address. Thereafter, I received an email from Manny in the February of 2011, asking if I could help him. I said yes and phoned him from England.

Clearly, one can see the remarkable set of events that brought us together. If I hadn't watched the TV documentary and contacted David and Pamela, following which she left David and went back to Sedona wherein she met Manny at the checkout, none of this would have happened (6). As for Manny, he had worked with some of the all-time greats of film, stage and music. Certainly, the list includes Rogers and Hammerstein, George Gershwin, Orson Wells and his best friend Bing Crosby. Indeed, the list goes on and on. All meaning, it was time for a psychic broadcaster to be added to his contacts.

Over the months that followed, we talked every day on the phone and built a close relationship. He told me of his ambition to have another Broadway hit: his last one being Sophisticated Ladies, which explored the life of Duke Ellington. However, he had told me he couldn't pay for my services, but he would sign me into his new production, a project also about Duke Ellington. During that year, Manny became very ill. One day, we were talking on the phone and he fell off a kitchen high stool onto a hard fall. I kept calling him, yet he didn't answer. So, trying to figure out what to do, I planned to use the internet to find the number of the emergency services in Sedona and call them from England. Thankfully, just as I was about to put the phone down, Manny answered me. He then called them for help himself. Overall, I felt helpless being thousands of miles away on the end of the phone.

Well, this was just the beginning of a series of illnesses Manny went through. I called the hospital every day and, fortunately, most days was able to speak to him. As an aside, I got to know his sons, Jon, Richard and Steve. In addition, his two brothers, Bernard (who is an award winning sound engineer with Universal Studios) and Charles (who is a prolific songwriter he wrote Killing Me Softly for Roberta Flack), became acquaintances.

By autumn Manny had recovered and wanted to meet. Moreover, around that time, he had started to write the script for his new production and had people in place—including members of the Duke's family—to get the show going. Clearly, Manny had been a close friend of Duke Ellington.

Manny had also told everyone about me. Thus, in the first week of December, I flew over to Arizona to meet Manny for the first time. Staggeringly, Jon, Manny's son, paid for my entire trip, including a limo to pick me up at Blue Harbour Airport in Phoenix and take me the 120 miles to Manny's home in Sedona. Unsurprisingly, the meeting was emotional. On top of which, it was Manny's 76th birthday on the 6th. Hence, due to everything Manny had mentioned, as well as the fall of his birthday, friends and family flew in from all over America. For his part, Jon and his friend Jay (whom I befriended) came in from New York, along with friends from Oregon, Chicago and Texas. We all had a great time, with Manny at the head of the dinner table, telling us about his life and all the people he had worked with, such as Marlon Brando, George Gershwin, the Marx Bros and Barbara Streisand. Additionally, this was an important meeting because an investor was present. All meaning, Manny secured the first monies for his show, even though a lot more was needed.

Taken together, I recorded five interviews with Manny at his home (7). Interestingly, they all reflect Manny's dream of us each being rich and famous. He even wanted Anne and me to move over to Sedona when the show was a success and build a home there. He had big plans and endless energy. I visited him again in January 2012, but little was I to know we wouldn't meet thereafter. Indeed, all was going well with preparations for the show until Manny was taken ill again. Thereafter, he was in and out of hospital. He had planned for the show to open on Broadway by the end of that year, yet it was not to be. Nowadays, his friend and lawyer, Bill Mortimer, is trying to get investments to revive the show as a legacy for Manny.

Manny rallied that August. He even made a trip to Beverley Hills, where his brother Charles lives, as well as his cousin, Cyrus Yavneh. Coincidentally, Cyrus is a Hollywood film producer with accreditations for the series *24* and *Supernatural*. In addition, his son, Steve, lived there and he stayed with him, his daughter-in-law and grandchildren. We continued to talk every day. He shared pictures with me of his time with them. One day, he had lunch with Charles and Cyrus telling them how I had helped him and how much his friendship with me meant to him. As a result, Cyrus wanted to talk to me, and I now speak every week on the phone to him. Moreover, when he came over to England for Christmas a year or so ago, Anne and I spent the day with him.

Following that, Manny flew home to Sedona, although he quickly became ill once more. Sadly, he had to be flown by helicopter to a hospital in Phoenix for life-saving heart surgery. He came through it. I would call the hospital every day, and the staff got to know me. Clearly, they were amazed I called so frequently from England. Again, he rallied and was moved to the hospital in Colindale. During his time there, his condition was up and down; some days he became incoherent. Contrarily, on 23rd September, a Sunday, I phoned him at 10 am Mountain time (6 pm over here in the UK) to find Manny bright and full of vigour. He said he felt great, had taken a shower, shaved and was fully dressed. Additionally, he was looking forward to his sons coming to visit him that afternoon; they had flown in to be with him because the overall signs for his health weren't good. Also, Bill and his daughter, Kristie, were going to visit him.

All meaning, the last words Manny spoke to me that day were: "Alan, I love you."

It was 6.30 am the next day in the UK when I was woken by a message from Bill saying Manny had passed away. He had had a great day with everyone. They left, he got undressed, got into bed and died peacefully. It was the end of an era. He was a man who gave me more than anything I could have given him. Furthermore, he showed me that one needs passion, as well as compassion, in life. Obviously, Manny visits me in spirit regularly. He is here as I write this and, thankfully, Bill sent me one of Manny's hats. He had a collection—look at media photos of him always wearing a hat. I will treasure it forever.

Indeed, we never know who we will meet in life. It doesn't matter if they are rich, poor or famous. The main thing is to love and care for them. Truly, strive for your goals, never give up and enjoy the journey. The world would be a better place if everyone did likewise. Eventually, we will take his last show on Broadway. Bill and I will strive until we succeed.

Little was I to know that my special friendship with Manny would lead to another special friendship with Cyrus Yavneh. As for Cyrus, this continues to date and has led to some great interviews on my radio show *Understanding Spirit*.

Chapter 18
Bishop David Parry

I now have to overlap my account of life's events in order for readers to get a clearer picture of what is happening on my journey. In November 2014, I was introduced to David Parry by our mutual friend, Gray Rudd. Now, Gray has always supported my work through my radio shows. Therefore, when Gray and David first met at the Paracon Convention in Derby (8), Gray talked about me and David said he had to get in touch with me. This he duly did by phone, although neither of us was aware what an incredible liaison would naturally arise. Certainly, David's long and illustrious career as a poet, author, spiritualist priest, theatre producer, director and actor was about to go one step further by being asked to become the first Valentinian (Gnostic) Bishop in England for at least 700 years. Indeed, this is as far as Church records go, because earlier documentation has been systematically destroyed by the enemies of freethinking.

Hence, David visited the church's headquarters in Italy to be consecrated. This took place in July 2015. By this time, of course, David and I had formed a great friendship, and he was in the process of introducing me to some amazing people from all walks of life. Thus, in August 2015, I was invited (through David) to go with him to the annual convention of the Ahmadiyya worldwide Muslim community in Hampshire, England. Stated so, from the moment we arrived, we were treated with the utmost respect and friendliness. Albeit, out of the 30,000 people attending, we were two of seven white people attending. Astonishingly, we met the Amir, and I learned a lot about them collectively. Sadly, they are shunned by many factions of the Muslim faith due to their work with people of different faiths, while encouraging everyone to respect and help each other.

Then in the November of 2015, David invited me to the annual convention of the Central Asian community in London. Among the guests was HRH Princess Katrina of Serbia, to whom David introduced me—a most gracious, friendly person, whom I was honoured to meet.

Overall, my friendship with Bishop David has equally allowed me to become a member of the Eurasian Creative Guild, which is a bringing together authors, actors and 94 dignitaries from across Eurasia into a working alliance, seeking to build bridges between Europe and these lands. Overall, it is a project masterminded by Marat Akhmedjanov, the owner of Hertfordshire Press, as well as Silk Road Media.

The next incredible event to happen while visiting him was David asking me if I would consider becoming the first Valentinian (Gnostic) Priest in England. I accepted immediately and, as a consequence, am now Reverend Father Alan Cox. Indeed, I was ordained on Easter Monday, 28th March 2016 (my birthday). Unexpectedly the businesswoman and now great friend Jillian Haslam insisted on paying for the venue and buying me my official ring: my seal of office. The ceremony was conducted in Dudley, West Midlands, by Bishop David whilst my family and close friends attended as witnesses. Some had travelled quite a distance to be there. Certainly, my thanks went out to the Rev. Sue Thompson, for being my official witness, along with her husband John.

What amazing friends I have! While all this was happening, David additionally asked if I would be advertising producer for a stage play called Shakespeare Tonight, which I accepted. The show went ahead on 1st to 6th August 2016 at the Theatro Technis, Camden, London—as part of the Camden Fringe Festival, thereafter touring to the Edinburgh Fringe Festival to play at Paradise in Augustine's theatre.

Chapter 19
The Hidden Enemy or Attracting Negative Energies

Have you ever wondered why some people always seem to be having so-called bad luck? Truly, we all have things that go awry from time to time (this is part of learning about ourselves and others—as well as how to deal with situations), yet there is a small group of people who attract negativity all the time. It seems there is one problem after another, and they draw the wrong kind of people to them. Well, this isn't just bad luck as one might think. Rather, these people are on a learning curve and continue to fail their lesson. In what way, one may ask? By way of explanation, let me say they fall into two categories: (a) those people who have done wrong in their past lives, or this life, and are being shown they need to alter their lifestyle; or (b) people who are a threat to the devil and his demonic helpers. Now, the first group can have their problems resolved by altering their day-to-day life pattern; i.e. choosing better company, along with the way they treat others. The second category is more difficult, because they have chosen, before being born, to pursue a life of trying to make the world a better place by helping people, animals, or both.

Of course, the devil will know those people who are vulnerable and the ones who have steel about them; individuals who cannot be dominated. Yes, I am saying 'dominated' since even though this person helps our 96 world, they may fail to recognise the signs of being drawn away from their true path by endless problems. Moreover, I know this second category from personal experience, having realised (early on) that I was being targeted by the devil myself. As such, he still tries, but by being strong and resolute, he has no powers over me. Indeed, it is we ourselves that allow him his so-called powers. Truly, he will send people into our lives whom he believes can cause us problems. Also, he will try to make us vulnerable through wrong decisions, such as spending recklessly so that we stop our true vocation by working to keep our head above water. Yet, even this is a smoke screen, because once one sits down to take stock, one can then put one's life into order and carry on. Indeed, that very old saying 'money is the root of all evil' is very close to the complete truth; either crimes are committed to obtain cash or an all-consuming pursuit of money can destroy someone's life. Other methods being: drugs, drink, criminal activities and wrongful sexual pursuits—clearly, anything perverting the mind to cause destruction of the person.

Now, here I am talking about the 'devil'—a word conjuring images of a creature resembling a man with red eyes, horns, a tail, and a long-handled two-pronged fork used to stoke the fires of hell—a horrible image. Yet, one's mind can become hell (or heaven). Hence, the trick is to take control of one's own mind and not allow the dark influences to control it. However, isn't this easier said than done? Well, it isn't as hard as you might think. First of all, one needs to recognise one has a problem. Deep down, of course, one knows when one does. All meaning, a point eventually comes when a window of light shows the way out of this situation. It is here where one needs to be strong. Some of us can decide then and there to start the road to recovery by ourselves; although others may need to seek help from a doctor, or specialised organisations, dealing with addictions. All good options, if one fits into those categories. But, there is another group that requires the direct approach of someone who can clear the devil and his demons away— someone who knows that a client's mind has been infiltrated to cause the grief. Curiously, people affected in this way can unknowingly bring out jealousy in others. Albeit correctly understood, they would see there is nothing to be jealous about, but instead grasp that a jealous person will only see what they want to see and will not believe the truth. This is when the work that I do comes into play. Obviously, I can't stop a person being jealous of anyone or prevent their destructive thoughts. Yet, with the partnership of my Spirit Guides, I can clear negative energies from the affected person's home or business.

Afterwards, placing a psychic barrier to free the person of other people's negative thoughts.

All explanations leading into example of what I have been talking about. A case in point, a lady both Anne and I know who has become a friend, as well as a client (9). Now, this lady's name is Penny Rollinson. She is an author who contributes to *Paranormal Galaxy* online digital magazine and someone who will be promoting her new book therein. Hence, anyone wanting to compare our accounts will be able to purchase Penny's book. Anyway, I received an email from Penny in the spring of 2012, asking for help. She had been in touch with David Ashworth, and he passed my contact information on to her because his work was by this time taking a different spiritual direction. Overall, he wasn't doing many clearings. So, when I spoke to Penny, she told me David had helped her ten years previously (clearing her old house of bad energies), which is why she approached him again. Therefore, we had a good long talk, afterwards agreeing Anne and I would drive down to her house in Wales—a trip of around 250 miles.

Once we arrived, we found she lived in a relatively new house—a property perhaps only ten years old. Moreover, it was situated in a private cul-de-sac with large, high electric gates, stopping anyone driving down the road to the five houses therein. All meaning, Penny's house was at the end of a short dead-end road. Certainly, it can't be seen from the main road and is only visible when one drives down to the very end of their road—laying back a good 30 feet from their next door neighbour. Thus, it was well secluded. On entering, I felt a great heaviness shrouding the house—a feeling similar to walking through treacle. What is more, these sensations were so heavy on my feet and head that it was psychically comparable to being compressed in a vice. Undeterred, we went through to the large kitchen where Penny said she spent a lot of her time, afterwards explaining how this bad energy came to her. Penny has a good knowledge of the Spirit World and knows that people can send bad energies to others. So, even though she lives alone, jealousy has occasionally reared its ugly head. Thence, the scene is set for the devil to work on Penny and bring the wrong man into her life. Certainly, everything had started when she went for a clairvoyant reading with a well-known so-called 'psychic' in

Bristol. Indeed, he was on tour there, and during the reading, she felt a strong attraction to him, which he reciprocated to her. Obviously, they met up a while later, having exchanged phone numbers. At first, their relationship blossomed and eventually he moved in with her. Possibly, I should say 'kind of moved in', since he spent long periods of time away doing his psychic work. Thoughtlessly, she gave him keys to the house in case she was at work when he returned from his travels. A move causing him to become controlling—particularly in subtle things, like questioning who she had as friends and where she was when he phoned her at night. Of course, elements of fear towards him emerged.

Curiously, Penny was in the process of writing a film script that she strongly felt would be a big success. She kept these writings on her laptop. A piece of equipment she left at home whence working. What is more, this work was complete and she was about to travel to Hollywood to present it to a film producer. Horrifyingly, when she went to use her laptop, she found all her work had been deleted, including her backup removable hard drive. Obviously, before their relationship had deteriorated, she shared her writings with him. For his part, he had copied it and then deleted five years' hard work. Unsurprisingly, he denied it, saying she must have deleted it herself, because she didn't understand computers. Well, this was the last straw. Penny found the inner courage to tell him to leave and not return. To add insult to injury (two years later), the film she had written was a box office smash hit. Yet, she had no proof whatsoever it was her story being told.

Following this, she contacted him to tell him what she thought of his despicable actions. Thereafter, bad energies started to work on her. Falling into a depression, she had the feeling of being alone and abandoned by family and friends. A few months later, she got her fight back and decided she needed to rid herself of all this negativity. After all, she thought what has happened has happened, and nothing will correct the wrong done to her. Meaning, of course, she had learnt her lesson and would not be so naive again. This is when she contacted Dave and then me.

Now, the kitchen was badly affected by these evil forces, which is why there was a strong smell of rotting cabbages; a common sign of demonic activity. Physically, of course, Penny's house is spotless. She keeps her home in pristine condition. There isn't a thing out of place, and a visitor wouldn't even know that she has two cats unless they saw them. Hence, this odious, putrid, smell made no logical sense other than being a common indication of demonic infestation. Thus, I linked into the bad energies, whilst my Spirit Guides helped me to locate the two demons hiding in the room. My guides (six at this point) surrounded the demons to stop them escaping—all allowing me to lock onto them. Then, with the help of my main guide, Ronaldo, we pulled and pushed them to the light. These demons were swearing at me, threatening me with the untold fury they would unleash in hell (10). Yet, the moment that they disappeared, the atmosphere lifted and the odious smell vanished. Therefore, the room became visibly lighter. A process having taken around ten minutes to complete, following which the rest of the rooms needed our attention.

Weirdly, along with demons come other negative entities. These are tiny black dots about the size of a nail on a little finger. What is more, these entities have tiny prongs on them—used to draw electrical energy in order to keep themselves in existence. Overall, they are the remnants of bad energy created over time by the bad things that happen in this world. One must remember, this stated, that all life (including the planet Earth itself) generates energy provided by the sun. Thus, it should come as no surprise that energies like these exist. When all said and done, the sun provides life, but it can equally destroy life. Hence, these entities have to be removed as well. A process sometimes taking longer than removing the demons, because there can be so many of them. Indeed, they affect the troubled person by draining their energy and making this person lethargic, thereby creating apathy at bedtime, which then prevents the person from sleeping properly, spending their nights tossing and turning.

Overall, the majority of the rooms had these entities in them, no demons. So, Anne and I, accompanied by Penny, went systematically clearing each area until we entered Penny's bedroom. Similar to downstairs in the kitchen, the atmosphere was heavy with that awful smell greeting us. Two more of these creatures were in there. Obviously, Anne helped to locate where they were hiding and when found, I removed them. Once a person becomes vulnerable to these negative energies, the floodgates can open and their personal space becomes completely infested. Either way, I don't feel there is a need for me to itemise all that was found; suffice to say there were many entities to be removed. Albeit, no more demons.

Clearly, every cleansing has to be complete. In which case, I link into the loft, or attic, as well as check the garage before leaving, not to mention any outbuildings and gardens, to make sure everything is done properly. All in all, it took over three hours, but the work was complete. Nowadays, Penny looks revitalised; the tired look has gone from her face. Furthermore, she says she hadn't felt this good for years. Meaning, of course, Anne and I left her in the knowledge that she could now begin to rebuild her life.

At the time all this was happening, I had got to know the Broadway producer Manny Fox. Now, Manny was looking for someone to write his life story and wanted it written in a way that told my story and how Manny met me. As such, I suggested Penny, and after he had talked to her on the phone, it was agreed that she would write the biography. The idea was that this book would be published to coincide with the opening of his Broadway show 'Sacred'. Sadly, with Manny dying, the project was put on hold until a time when we could get the show moving again. Looking back, we three had regular chats regarding how the book should be written, what format it would take, the most important thread of the story and so on. As for Manny, he thought it could focus on how he and I came together—an event giving him the energy to create the show. I recall Manny and I spending hours talking about how the production should be done, with Bill Mortimer playing a major part in the development.

However, I digress. Overall, I thought it necessary to explain the significance of Penny's psychic attacks, as well as the way they manifested. This is because of her vital contribution to the potential success of the show. Anyway, Penny had written two chapters that Manny and I had received for approval. A professional courtesy paid to us both. Thereafter, she had started on the third chapter when Manny sadly passed away. At this point, it would appear that the evil energies had won, stopping everything to do with the development of the show. Yet, this was not the case. Rather, Bill and I knew the show had to continue. Especially, after so much effort has been put into it. Moreover, we wanted a legacy to honour this great man's work. Hence, Penny still continues to write this joint biography.

Currently, almost 12 months to the day after these psychic attacks, a new set of demons and entities have begun to attack Penny, this time manifesting themselves from an entirely different quarter. Indeed, these attacks were coming from two people that Penny would have trusted with her life. Two people who showed their real intentions through careless actions and words. Stated so, things had started to go wrong for her again. She was made redundant from her job, her pets suddenly became ill and people she knew acted distant towards her. Following which, she called Anne and me for a second time to clear her home and herself. Astonishingly, when Anne and I arrived, it was like a replica of the first clearing. Additionally, when someone gets psychically attacked twice, a DNA pattern is occasionally created from the first attack. Thereafter, other bad energies can use it to work on their victim. Truly, 99% of people cleared do not have this legacy, but anyone the devil sees as a threat (and who has a psychic investigator) is affected in this way. At which point, it is then possible for hidden connections to evil to be uncovered. Please remember when clearing bad energies it isn't like clearing blocked water pipes, or mending a broken object. Instead, one is dealing with sly and cunning beings. Thusly, it can take time to get things right. Also, the victim has to help themselves by altering their lifestyle and/or disassociating themselves from problematic people. Although, everything can't be solved by a clearing alone, and the victim in question needs to take some responsibility for their recovery.

Admittedly, Penny cut the two people, who had been psychically attacking her, out of her life. Meanwhile, the psychic protection that I, with my guides, put in place, stopped any more bad energies coming through. A couple of times these people tried to come back into her life, but Penny didn't respond. Indeed, if she had done so, a connection would have been re-established and their negative influence resumed. In any case, the clearing was completed successfully. Speedily, she found a new job with better pay, as well as greater responsibility and autonomy.

Life went well for another 12 months, until she was introduced to a man at a charitable event; a man who was a lot older than Penny and married. Certainly, their connection was nothing to do with any physical attraction. In fact, there wasn't one. He just purported to be a nice guy who wanted to help Penny once he had discovered she lived alone and needed odd jobs done. Over the following few months, he volunteered to do work for her while she was away from home working. Unthinkingly, she agreed and gave him a key. Now, he was trustworthy in the sense that he never took anything from the house, yet he found jobs that may or may not have been necessary and then expected payment for them. Eventually, Penny noticed (after being away through the working week) that as she entered the house, she went down in herself—feeling very negative and irritated. Furthermore, her cats started to become ill. Unsurprisingly, Penny told the man she felt he was bringing this negativity into her home and didn't want him to come back. For his part, he said he would return her key, when she was away, by giving it to her neighbour, along with some tools he had borrowed. Oddly, he did accept he had bad energy with him. In addition, when Penny told him that over a period of three or four weeks she had tried to get him to be cleared, he didn't say he was all right. So, when Penny finally said she wanted him to keep away from her, he exhibited no surprise at all.

Obviously, I was asked to return for a third time to clear her house and herself, which I dutifully did. Again, the clearing process was similar; removing some demons and entities. When completed, I explained to Penny that she was being attacked because she was too open with people. It was a lesson she needed to learn. Clearly, it is good to be friendly with people, yet not too eager to tell someone everything about you; it takes time to build a good friendship. Thinking ahead, it will be very interesting to read Penny's account of the clearings and how she felt afterwards. After all, Penny has become a friend, as well as a client. All meaning, we wish her every success in the future.

Chapter 20
Healing Animals

In this regard, a couple of instances readily come to mind. For example, my sister in law, Lynne Compton, had a lovely horse named H, although he has sadly passed away. He was a Dapple Grey Belgian Warm Blood cross-country hunting horse. On one of the previous owner's country jaunts, a twig went (and lodged) into his left eye, causing him to lose his sight. As such, he was no longer wanted because he couldn't perform his duties. Now, H was greatly loved by Lynne. She gave him the best attention it was possible to give. Indeed, he was kept at a good stabling yard, while Lynne attended him at least twice every day, spending quality time with him. However, one day when she was riding H, he went down a small hole in the field near the stables and damaged his digi-flex tendon. This is the tendon in the ankle that controls the hoof and when this happens—depending on the severity of the damage—a horse is usually put down, because it can't support itself. An operation may be attempted, but there is no guarantee it will be successful and would cause huge stress for the animal.

So, knowing I heal people through Spirit, Lynne asked if I would go to the stables and see if healing, or psychic surgery, would help H. After all, she was not going to give up on him. Thus, I went to the stables with Lynne to see if he could be psychically helped. In himself, H was a lovely gentle horse who seemed to sense I was there to try and help him.

Hence, I entered his stable saying, "Hello," as well as I would try and take his pain away to help him walk.

Obviously, horses can be unpredictable, and I was aware that he might kick me with his hind legs if he didn't like me touching him. Yet, I needn't have worried, since he stood perfectly still for around half an hour, allowing me to gently put my hands around his ankle. Indeed, as I was sitting on the stable floor beside of him, I could feel the energy through my hands going into H's ankle. There was a strange 'feeling of things' (the only way I can describe it) inside his leg as if tendons were being mended or repositioned.

Fascinatingly, when the surgeon in spirit had finished his work on H, I felt my hands being released from his leg—although, up until then, they seemed glued in position to allow this work to be done. Eventually, I got up from the floor feeling stiff and wondering if I needed healing to recover from sitting in the same position for that length of time. Anyway, I went round to H on the side of his good eye and said to him that I hoped that would help. What happened next was beautiful; H swiftly moved his head round towards me, just stopping short of the side of my face. Then, ever so gently, he put this side of his head against my left cheek and held it there. This was his way of saying 'thank you'. I felt emotional through the fact H wanted to show how much it meant to him.

As time passed (and with strapping on his lower leg for extra support), H was able to lead a fairly normal life. Lynne's days of being able to ride H had obviously gone, the risk to him being too great. But, he was only left with a weakness in that leg. Overall, he wasn't in any real pain. Thusly, he lived happily for another 15 years after this episode in his life.

Around the same time as I helped H, a lady called Jayne contacted me after having found out about me from a friend of hers whom I had given healing. Now, Jayne owned four horses and was a successful horse rider. Indeed, she travelled the country competing at all the major show jumping events. Her favourite horse being an Apache, which had hurt his left side in a freak accident inside his stable enclosure. Moreover, Jayne herself was recovering from a fall from one of her other horses. By this time, I sensed I had an affinity with horses, so I gave healing by gently placing my hands on the horse's side—as the animal stood perfectly still. When I had finished, the horse did exactly the same thing that H had done; his head came round towards my face very quickly, then stopped and gently rested against my cheek, leaving it there for several moments before giving out a loud neigh. Jayne said she hadn't witnessed anything like that before in all her ten years of being involved with horses. Additionally, she asked if I could help her with her own left arm; it was causing her discomfort following the time she had broken it while falling from one of her other horses. Unfortunately, she had broken the same arm four times through falling off horses. Hence, it was now difficult for her to ride, since she couldn't lift it above shoulder level due to the pain. So, I took hold of her lower arm just above her wrist. Moments later, Jayne and I felt powerful movements within her arm. Amazingly, all of the bones were moving very quickly; it felt like they were being realigned into their correct position. Afterwards, Jayne said the feeling was not one of pain but relief, as if a great pressure was lifted. Interestingly, this went on for about two minutes, where after the movement suddenly stopped.

I then released Jayne's arm saying, "How does that feel now?"

She held her arm with her hand and said it felt light and pleasantly normal. What is more; she lifted her left arm right up into the air above her head with no effort at all, rotating it with ease. Personally, I had never experienced anything like that before—feeling bones knitting back into place; it was quite surreal. Nevertheless, I had two happy customers; the horse and Jayne. Certainly, I didn't hear from her again. Therefore, I assume she managed to stay mounted on future outings and didn't break anymore bones.

On a related note, a number of years ago, Anne and I regularly attended a Friday indoor antiques market in the town of Leek, Staffordshire—a market town which lies 40 miles north of our home. We had a stall there selling jewellery and crystals. Every week, therefore, we would see the same faces coming to find out if stallholders were offering anything new. Two of these people we got to know by having a chat each time they visited. They were mother and daughter, Joanne Hayes and Kerri. Now, Anne and I learned they were great animal lovers. Indeed, Jo rescued unwanted, cruelly treated greyhounds, while Kerri rescued racehorses. All animals were about to be put down for no other reason than they were not earning their keep for their racing stables. Interestingly, both of their husbands supported them in their quest as much as they could within financial bounds.

As a case in point, Kerri said she had just taken delivery of a mare she had named Nyella. A statement explained by the fact that Kerri has a friend who lived in Ireland running a rescue charity for unwanted horses. As such, she was told by a stable girl that this particular horse had been badly treated—having witnessed it being beaten when the mare wouldn't do as its owner wanted; one of the main causes for these beatings being the horse's reluctance to go into a horsebox for transport. Horrifyingly, it was due to go for slaughter when Kerri's friend stepped in and bought the horse in order to save it. So, during a phone conversation between Kerri and her friend, they arranged transport to bring Nyella over to England. For her part, Kerri went over to Ireland to oversee the transportation. However, when trying to load Nyella into the horsebox, it was obvious she was terrified. Clearly, Nyella kicked violently and raised herself high into the air to prevent being put inside. Overall, it took over an hour to get her loaded; everyone waited until the horse ran out of stamina, whence they were able to persuade her into the box. On top of this, the journey back to England was traumatic for the horse. It took nearly two hours to drive to the ferry port, following which there was a half hour wait for the ferry to sail. Obviously, Kerri had tried to time it so there wouldn't be a long wait at the ferry terminal, thereby eliminating as much stress as possible for Nyella. Certainly, Kerri didn't dare unload the horse for exercise in case she couldn't get it back into the box. Nonetheless, it took two hours for the crossing to Holyhead (on the isle of Anglesey), which is adjoined to the mainland of Wales by two road bridges. Thereafter, another long journey of about four hours to Kerri's stables ensued. As one can imagine, Nyella was not a happy horse. Eventually, of course, Kerri and her husband took the trailer into an exercise field in order to unload Nyella, while taking care not to get kicked in the process. Indeed, they let her run maniacally around the field to release her frustration.

After two hours, she had settled down to grazing. So, Kerri took the opportunity—with the help of a couple of other horse owners—to take her to her new stable pen. A month passed and Nyella was beginning to settle in, even though she was still aggressive. At which point, on one of Kerri and Jo's visits to the market, Kerri asked if I would be able to go to Nyella and see if healing would help. I agreed to go and see what could be done. Thus, four days later, I drove up to the stable yard to meet Kerri and Jo, in order to assist Nyella. Now, as I entered the stables, inquisitive horses either side of me were eager to see a new face enter their space. After all, apart from being noisy, horses are a lot more intelligent than people realise. Anyway, I arrived at the forth stall on the left where Nyella was housed. She looked up to see who had come to visit her. For her part, Kerri said she would enter the stall first to keep her calm. As I stated earlier, horses are my favourite animals even though I love all animals. Yet, I would be lying if I said I had no fear of them. They are large, imposing animals that could do a lot of damage, and I wasn't feeling secure with Nyella, since I knew her history. Nevertheless, Kerri closed the stall gate behind her to stop Nyella making a dash for freedom, which she had done before. Upon Kerri's invitation to enter the stall, however, I slowly opened the gate so as not to startle the mare. Kerri then moved to the front of Nyella, and I went to the left hand side of the horse. She had a problem with her side and rear quarters. So, I gently put both my hands onto Nyella's side and rested them there to allow the healing energy to flow through me from the doctor in spirit. I could feel the tenderness inside her. Furthermore, the energy from within my hands was pulsating through into her. At first, all was well as Nyella stood there. Kerri was talking to her, reassuring her that everything was okay. Then, suddenly, Nyella swung her head round and nipped me quite hard on my left arm. It was unexpected and even through the coat I was wearing it hurt. However, this was not going to stop me from helping her, although Kerri thought I should leave the stall for my own safety. Yet, I had a strong feeling I should continue, which I did. Now, I was expecting more trouble from Nyella, but she seemed to realise I was trying to help her. She didn't bite me again, even though she obviously wasn't comfortable with the situation. Be that as it may, Dr Ingles (in spirit) kept my hands firmly stuck onto Nyella for another ten minutes, until he had finished his work. Kerri and I then left Nyella to recover from the experience.

Some time passed. About three months later, Kerri got in touch with me again to say Nyella had calmed down rapidly after that day. Her aggression had gone almost immediately. What is more, Kerri said Nyella was interacting with the other horses in a positive way. Indeed, the vet had even commented he could see a remarkable improvement in her severe injuries in a very short period. Also, Kerri had moved stables to another yard and needed to transport Nyella by using the horsebox trailer, but on this occasion she went into it with ease; no kicking, or rearing up, or neighing. Indeed, she followed Kerri inside and stood there, waiting for the trailer to be moved. Moreover, once they arrived at her new home, she just gently backed out of the horsebox and went into the surrounding field to look at her new surroundings. All is still well for Nyella. Kerri says that Nyella is now enjoying life.

A few years onwards and Kerri, along with Jo, have kept in touch through social media. Furthermore, before starting to write this book, I had a message from Jo asking if I could help her three rescued greyhounds, especially Lily, who had been badly treated by her previous owner. Overall, she had been beaten on her side, meaning, it hurt her to lie down. Now, usually when a stranger arrives at a house wherein dogs reside, there is a lot of barking and commotion. However, this was not so at Jo's house. When attending, therefore, I went through to the living room to find all three greyhounds lying down with no interest in who had entered the room. Sadly, Jo said the dogs had been like this since she got them. Lily, for instance, was lying on her left side—the side that was alright. Yet, she looked uncomfortable, causing Jo to say Lily wouldn't let any man (including Jo's husband) near her. In herself, Lily was a grey-flecked-coated greyhound, who looked tired and fed up with life. All meaning, Jo probably needed to hold Lily for me. Curiously, there was no need as Lily just lay there once I told her I wanted to make her pain go away. She seemed to understand and let me gently put my hands on her good side, so the healing energy would go through her body. After about thirty minutes, the healing was over and Lily got up, wagged her tail and went over to Jo for a cuddle. Jo said she wouldn't have believed it if she hadn't seen with her own eyes. Obviously, I thank Doctor Ingles for the calming influence he had on Lily and the work he performed on her. Afterwards, there was a visible improvement in Lily's demeanour. She had a twinkle in her eyes. Following this, it was Eric's turn to experience the energy boost from Doctor Ingles through my hands.

Hence, I shuffled on my bottom over to him and said, "Hello, Eric, can I place my hands gently on you please? Just here on your back?"

Amazingly, as I spoke these words to him, he put his head back down on the bed and let me get on with it. Eric is a lovely quiet soul, with a black and white shiny coloured coat. Clearly, he had been through a lot in his life, but now was enjoying some quality time with Jo caring for him. He let me touch him for about 15 minutes or so, then suddenly got up and walked over to Jo as if to say that's enough now.

I then went over to Gem, an all-black, laid-back greyhound that, in all fairness, was not in need of much help; she seemed the one of the three dogs that was all right. Nonetheless, Doctor Ingles gave her some energy through my hands to help her. The whole session lasted for about two hours, and all three greyhounds are doing well nowadays. Indeed, Lily's side has recovered and is no longer in pain, whilst Eric and Gem are full of natural vitality.

Chapter 21
Psychic Surgery

Healing and psychic surgery have been with us since man first walked on Earth. Over the centuries, it was considered to be witchcraft, since people were afraid of its inexplicable results. Indeed, many healers were put to death by those who did not understand! Yet, as time went by, a more tolerant attitude to healing developed, and the persecution stopped. Thus, it was acknowledged and known as faith healing.

Today, most people have a better understanding of healing and realise it is a universal God-given energy that is there for us all to tap into. As such, I have been blessed with a connection to help people in this way. Below, therefore, are examples of healing and psychic surgery. I must state I do not take credit for the examples outlined. Rather, I am a vessel, or conduit, for God's energy, as it courses through me from doctors in spirit.

So, going back to 2008, Anne and I were featured in *Take a Break: Fate and Fortune* magazine, one of the top monthly mainstream magazines in the UK. However, a week before the photographer came to our home to do the photo-shoot, I was asked (at the last minute) to do psychic readings at a hotel in a small village in Worcestershire. It seemed one of the readers was ill and couldn't attend; all marking the first part of these unexplained happenings.

On arrival, my first client was a young lady.

She was a lovely, bubbly person, and I began the reading by saying, "You know you have health issues, and you are determined to get well."

Surprised, she then told me she had been given six months to live because of aggressive cancer in her liver, kidneys and stomach. I put my left hand on her right lower arm, after asking if I could do this. Immediately, she said she felt a surge of intense energy go up her arm and down into her stomach, back and side. She said she literally felt energised. As a result, she asked me if I would go to her home the following week to give her more healing, to which I agreed. This was in November, whereas, she had been diagnosed in August. Moreover, the meeting at the hotel took place on a Tuesday evening, while that coming Saturday, the photo-shoot took place.

Now, the photo-shoot went well, and just as the photographer was about to leave, he said he had an important day on Monday. He was following a young lady who had terminal cancer, although she was determined to beat it. Indeed, she was going to tell her story each week in *Take a Break* magazine—the sister weekly publication to the one we were being featured in. Instantly, Anne said to him that we had met a young lady in Worcestershire, who we were trying to help and, if it was appropriate for him to tell this person about me, we would see if she could be helped.

The photographer said, in an incredulous voice, the name of this lady and we said, "Yes, it's her we are helping."

So the photographer lived in Warwickshire, the lady lived in Worcestershire and I lived in Staffordshire; making a perfect 40-mile triangle between all of us.

The following week, I went to the young lady's home, and she had psychic surgery. I placed my hand on her stomach, and she immediately said she thought my hand had gone inside her. Startlingly, she felt her insides being pulled and tugged about, but without pain. It was the doctor in spirit, Dr David Ingles, doing his work. This went on for around an hour. However, the strange thing is I don't feel anything while this work is going on and cannot physically move my hand until it is complete. Obviously, she asked me to return the following week, although this time the healing was gentler and not so intense. She said she felt energised and could do more in the daytime.

Christmas came, and she went down with a very heavy flu. Overall, she was in bed for two weeks and at low ebb. Yet, she recovered in time to go for a pre-arranged hospital appointment and had a scan. At this point, she said she felt great, no pain and loads of energy. Astonishingly, the scan revealed that all the cancer had gone. No trace anywhere in her body. The consultant and doctors had no explanation for this. She is now enjoying her life to the full.

Now, the other amazing thing about all this is she was going through a tough time in her marriage. She had two very young children, even though her husband didn't support her at all through her illness. Thus, the first thing she did after her recovery was to end her marriage. Indeed, she felt liberated and went back to her job, which was working with vulnerable children. Here, of course, is a series of events that cannot be explained except in a spiritual way. After all, I shouldn't have been at that hotel that evening, but everything was pre-arranged by God, or Spirit. In this mysterious manner, such connections are meant to be.

Conclusion

This world of ours is full of surprises; some good, some bad. However, the bad seem to have an immediate impact on people, and it takes a long time for justice to be done against perpetrators. As such, I have pondered this reality for many years. Why it is like this if God is all powerful and all knowing? Why does He allow such atrocities that occur on a daily basis on Earth? My conclusion is that people must be given the ability to decide their own actions and it is we that have to account for our deeds—not God.

Indeed, the criminal or moral wrong doer appears to get away with their actions before justice is seen to be done. Meanwhile, this can be very frustrating and hurtful to the victims, their friends and family. What is more; why do so many people (sometimes hundreds and thousands of innocents) get harmed or killed in wars they didn't want any involvement in. Clearly, one learns (almost daily) through TV screens, as well as in newspapers or on radios, of atrocities committed in the name of God by subversives, or fanatics, who believe that their way is the only way. Moreover, the Western world goes from one conflict to another trying to stop this carnage, because not to do so would cause even more destruction. It is the same principle on a personal basis. If one is attacked and the perpetrator is allowed to get away, thereafter they will continue hurting others. Hence, it seems we need to fight the good fight to defeat the evil ones. Now, this in itself is controversial to some people. How can it be right to kill another human being, while trying to stop them killing others, they say? Well, what is the alterative—do nothing and allow those people who want to rule the world to do so by their evil actions? Sadly, sometimes it isn't possible to 'turn the other cheek' since the other side will not listen to reason. That is my view anyway. Readers might disagree, but

I can respond by saying what would our world be like if Adolph Hitler hadn't been stopped? Obviously, one needs to ask what this has to do with spirituality and clearing demons, or bad entities. In actual fact, it has to do with everything because what happens here is linked to the spiritual realms. Furthermore, bad things happening on Earth are connected to Satan. Of course, this doesn't mean each evil occurrence is down to the devil. Certainly, just as God isn't responsible for our wrong doings, neither is the devil. Yet, God helps us (collectively) to find a solution to bad deeds, whilst the devil tries to find a way to make those bad deeds have the worst possible effect. In both cases, it's up to us to do the right thing.

Overall, I have battled with the devil so many times since awakening to my spiritual journey. Moreover, he has targeted me as well as attacked Anne to try and get me to stop helping people. Be that as it may, she, like me, will never give up the fight against evil. After all, a calling becomes a way of life. I say this hoping not to sound too pious or egotistical. It is just what I have to do. Thus, the accounts given in this book are the most memorable and dramatic that I can recall. Albeit, there are many more that Anne and I have experienced. Please remember if anyone is going through a terrible time, then there is a good chance bad spirits are making things worse. Nevertheless, help is at hand, and there are good people who can help. Don't ever believe that there isn't a way out of a situation. All one needs to do is face up to the troubling circumstances and deal with them appropriately. It's the only way to free oneself from the devil's grip.

Stated so, there was a time in my life when I neglected my spiritual path. However, it seems God had this part of my life planned out for me, and I am more than happy to follow Him. I am not a 'church person' as such, and my aim isn't to convert people to the way I think. Indeed, whatever way one sees life is one's choice, so whoever comes my way for help can get it without fear of conversion. My aim is that we can all get on with our lives and find our own direction in joy.

At the end of the day, I hope you have found this book a good read; entertaining and informative. This is my first attempt, and it is a very singular experience to sit down and put one's thoughts and feelings into words. In some ways, it has been very therapeutic. Undoubtedly, my journey continues, and who knows what adventures await me. By adventures, of course, I mean what awaits me each and every day of my life. After all, if one looks at life correctly, every day of one's life is an adventure. Thence, as some people go to clairvoyants to get a glimpse of the future, I like to take each day as it comes, with my hopes, wishes and goals in mind.

A Reflective Afterword by David Parry

Writing the afterword to a book is never easy. Especially in matters esoteric. However, as a close personal friend of Fr. Alan Cox, as well as his editor, the honour of rounding off this autobiographical essay has fallen to me. A task, in light of the unusual material, proving to be more difficult than I initially thought. After all, even though a Spiritualist myself, I tend to see these recondite subjects as part of our Western theological tradition. That is, in terms of interior and exterior experience—or phrased alternatively, in the inherited categories of Existence and Monadology.

Now, a monad (the subject of Monadology), considered as vocabulary and idea, has been outlined by various authors, including that colossus of philosophy and mathematics Gottfried Leibniz (1646–1716). Indeed, in Leibniz's writings, he describes them as a 'unit of consciousness' or 'a simple substance'. So, if understood by the word 'souls', it seemed to him their basic order was three-tiered: (1) entelechies or created monads, (2) souls or entelechies with perception and memory, and (3) spirits or rational souls. Hence, whatever is said about the lower orders (entelechies) is valid for the higher (souls and spirits) but not vice versa. Furthermore, as none of them is without a 'body', there is a corresponding hierarchy of (1) living beings and animals, (2) non-reasonable or (3) reasonable entities. Each degree of perfection corresponding to cognitive abilities, whilst only spirits, or reasonable animals, are able to grasp the ideas of both the world and its Creator. As such, some monads have power over others because they can perceive with greater clarity, even though, one monad may be said to dominate another if it contains the reasons for the actions of others. On top of which, Leibniz believed that anybody (animal or human) has one dominant monad which controls the others within it. Indeed, Leibniz surmised there are indefinitely many substances individually 'fated' to act in a predetermined way: each substance being coordinated with all the others. To me personally, therefore, Monadology (understood as Spiritualism) is the most demanding of intellectual undertakings—a study looking at the inner dynamics of consciousness as well as outside at related physical phenomena.

From the outside, of course, this extended essay traces the steps of a naturally gifted psychic who flowered as a radio broadcaster. A man of humble origins, who nonetheless found he could 'tune in' to rarefied dimensions of experience, at the same time as delighting his audiences by discussing these specialised topics with like-minded guests on his highly acclaimed show. With this in mind, *The Life of a Psychic Broadcaster* will equally outrage and astonish its readers with tales of astral surgery, exorcism, near miraculous healings and preternatural encounters with reptilian entities. Quite apart from recounting Alan Cox's dealings with the great and the gay among A-list celebrities. Hence, the mysteries of inside and outside continue to 'haunt' a topic proven to be the most complicated of all human interests throughout recorded history. All in all, I heartily recommend this book to anyone seeking to know more about this life, along with the hereafter.

London, 2017.

End Notes

- Have a listen by going to www.paramaniaradio.com
- His films are numerous; it would take a separate essay to include them all. You can listen to Chris's interview with me via my website www.calmingthoughts.com where a podcast is available there.,
- Authorities later discovering the car had been stolen earlier that day.
- Channel 4 was a ground-breaking medium for British television.
- Now Pamela Leigh Richards.
- If one search engines Manny Fox Broadway Producer, one can read about the incredible career he had.
- The first one went out live on www.paramaniaradio.com as one of my shows Understanding Spirit, where he told his life story. The shows can be listened to via my website www.theworldtoheal.com and on demand at www.paramaniaradio.com
- The first Paracon convention in our UK took place in Derby 2014 and was initiated by the American serviceman Matt Hall.
- She is writing a book and says she will be telling her own story of how I have helped her. When learning this only a few days ago (21 June 2014), I said to her I was going to ask if I could write her story. However, if she was going to give an account of what happened over the past three years perhaps I should not. Interestingly, her reaction was to say I should give my version, because it will be different from hers and

will give people reading both accounts a better understanding of her situation.

- Over the years, I have heard these threats from these creatures that have never walked this earth; so I will take my chances in the knowledge that each demon removed is one less performing their vile deeds on people.

Appendix 1

My work takes me all over the UK, as well as other countries like America. As such, I have travelled extensively in order to help people who have the misfortune of suffering from negative energies. In this respect, one story instantly comes to mind from four or five years ago, when I went to help someone in Dagenham, London. Indeed, while exhibiting at a Mind, Body and Spirit exhibition, I was approached by one of the other exhibitors who said he and his family were being attacked in their home by 'scary energies'. Things were literally going bump in the night. Hence, a happy home had been turned into a family arguing all the time over nothing. They were tired in the day, but couldn't sleep at night. This was particularly worrying, because the husband of this household was in the fire brigade. All meaning, lives depended on him being focused. He asked, therefore, if I would visit his home to remove these bad spirits.

On my arrival, I entered this property to the feeling of a strong negative presence. So, I set to work with the help of my Spirit Guides. Well, during this process, I was drawn to their bathroom—finding out afterwards that this was where most of the problems occurred. Indeed, I felt the presence of a demon. Of course, these creatures haven't ever lived like us. However, their sole purpose is to try and destroy us human beings by affecting our daily lives in a negative way. Shockingly, they try to make us feel we have no way to progress, while trying to ruin our activities. Yet, they have no real powers. All they can do is work on our minds and, once confronted by someone who has the ability to remove them, go away because they are cowards. After all, they can't fight and win against God's energy.

Now, this was a particularly nasty demon. It entered my body and I felt sick. Moreover, it tried to talk through me by changing my voice to a harsh, deep, sinister, tone. Confessedly, I have had this happen on three occasions, although my guides protected me and instantly removed them. Afterwards, I was able to send it to the spiritual light, where on the whole atmosphere in the room, not to mention the house, changed. Instead of oppression, there was now a feeling of light and happiness. The whole process, from arriving to completing the cleansing, took around two hours.

I heard from the family a few weeks later. Harmony and normality had returned to them all. They were sleeping well and getting on with their lives with no pointless arguments.

Appendix 2

Another fascinating incident happened in the week between Christmas day and the New Year in 2004. Back then, I was asked to go to a house in Wolverhampton to do clairvoyant readings for six people. An event wherein everything went well, certainly, everyone there that afternoon enjoyed themselves and the readings were well-received.

Now, the last person to come into the room while I was doing these private readings was Michael. He sat down opposite me, with the dining table between us, and I switched on the recorder so he could take a copy away with him. I did this for all of my readings. Stated so, I always start these readings by saying my name and giving a date. Thereafter, making the statement that readings are for entertainment purposes only; this is a legal requirement to protect vulnerable people hanging on a clairvoyant's every word. In any case, I agree it is a good thing to do whether it's law or not. Following this, I would then play this beginning part back to make sure the recording was audible.

Please remember this was the last of the six readings, and there hadn't been an issue with all the other five recordings. Thus, when I started the playback, everyone was shocked that the voice coming out of the speaker was not of this world. Indeed, the words were not mine; the voice was deep, dark, and menacing. Moreover, it was difficult for Michael and me to understand every word. However, the message 127 was clear: 'leave well alone.' Obviously, I had no idea who I was dealing with. Anyway, it didn't scare me even though I knew this was the devil.

Michael looked at me starkly and then said, "I was going to ask you if you could see what was happening to me, but you now know. I am being attacked by demons and the devil; can you help me, please?"

Hence, I arranged to visit his home, where he lived alone with his pet dog, near Shrewsbury, Shropshire. Clearly, the house was a typical English country cottage that one would see on the lid of a tin of biscuits. Either way, on entering, Michael said he had locked his dog, Jake (a black and white coated cross collie), in one of the bedrooms in fear it would attack me. This was one of the many things over the past two months that had drastically altered Michael's life. He said he had this dog since it was a puppy; he was now seven years old and had always been a loving and gentle dog with no signs of aggression towards anyone. Yet, the dog had turned on Michael and bitten him on his leg on two occasions in the past week. The change had come about after the visit of an unexpected person to his house asking for Michael's help. Now, Michael was clairvoyant and although he tried to help the woman, he sensed she was very angry: she left muttering indistinguishable words under her breath. During the two months after this visit, Michael had lost his job unexpectedly, as well as developed an illness that left him with no energy. His doctor couldn't find the cause of it and put it down to fatigue through over-work, while his pet dog had become like a rabid animal.

On top of this, the cottage had a very heavy atmosphere. It felt like walking through treacle, while the tell-tale smell of rotting cabbages hung in the air. His home was clean with no out of date food anywhere around. These occurrences are not unusual, however, when a house is infested with demons and bad entities. I said to Michael I would go around his house to locate and remove these unwanted evil beings; I asked him to accompany me so he would feel their presence gone. There were three demons and seven entities in the downstairs living room and kitchen. After linking in, I sent them to the light with the help of my Spirit Guides. Moreover, I saw in my mind's eye the atmosphere throughout the cottage altering dramatically. The heavy feeling disappeared, and the awful stench of rotting vegetables had gone; the rooms now felt light and airy. Following this, we went upstairs. The first door on the right— on the landing—was shut; all the others were left wide open. Inside, the dog barked aggressively. At this point, one may think I had lost my marbles and taken leave of my senses; I said to Michael to unlock the door and open it so I could go in and clear what was in there.

He looked at me and said, "No! It's too dangerous; he will attack you!"

I said he wouldn't do that; the words came out of my mouth, but it was if someone else was saying them. Clearly, it was my guide Ronaldo talking through me. So, against Michael's better judgment, he unlocked and opened the door to the bedroom. Therein, the dog was sitting bolt upright on the floor between the bed and the dressing table about nine feet into the room; he had stopped barking as the door was being opened. He was now growling very quietly; his stare was transfixed on me as I entered the room first before Michael—who had moved back out on to the landing. I walked slowly into the room towards the snarling dog and started to talk to him.

I can't remember the exact words I said, but it was something on the lines, "I have come to help you and your master; I know you don't want to hurt me. You are scared and you don't know why you have become angry."

Then, I put my right hand gently on to the dog's head and placed my thumb and forefinger together gently. Thereby, quickly pulling the demon from within him out and sending it to the light. The dog changed instantly. He wagged his tail furiously and brushed his body next to my legs in an effort to show his thanks for helping him. Afterwards, I went into the other two bedrooms and bathroom to remove the remainder of the bad energies with the dog following me everywhere still wagging his tail. Michael was astounded at the transformation of his beloved pet. Finally, we all went downstairs, and I asked Michael if he would like some healing from me for his injured leg. Overall, it was healing but still giving pain because the bite had gone deep through to the bone. Michael sat down in his armchair with his foot resting on a low level stool. I put my hand on his leg; meanwhile, the dog was watching intently and came alongside his master to put his paw onto Michael's leg close to mine—which stayed there for the entire time I was doing the healing. When I had finished, the dog removed his paw and also looked at me. It licked my face then jumped onto his master's lap, thereafter licking Michael before settling down on him. Michael said he was trying to understand the incredibly positive changes that had just happened. He said he had got his best friend back again, having been frightened he would have to have him put to sleep in case he bit anyone else. Yet, he was back to the pet he knew and loved. Looking back, I had a phone call from Michael about a month later saying that all was well and he had a new job. Moreover, he had started that week. It was better than the one he had lost, while his dog was still as loving towards him. Indeed, he also had a new lady in his life. All early days, but the dog liked her; so everything was good.

When sudden bad changes happen, it is a strong possibility that the devil is at work. However, he can be defeated once it is recognised that unholy forces are operative.

Appendix 3
My Connection with Jillian Haslam

I thought I had completed my book last year, but how wrong could I have been. The deadline for completion was September 2014. Indeed, this book seemed completed by the end of June so it would be ready for publication. Then, a series of events happened, which I can't go into concerning another person, which transpired in the launch being delayed. I know why now. God and Spirit work in incredible ways because it transpires that I hadn't finished my book after all.

Anyway, on 29 May, 2015, my life was about to change for the better; that day Anne and I met Jillian Haslam for the first time. Overall, the meeting had been arranged by Spirit a year before without anyone's knowledge here on Earth. This is how Spirit works. Indeed, sometime in 2014, I received an email from a lady in India that I now know as Goldi. I can't remember the date she contacted me, although that in itself is an oddity because I diligently write all my clients down in my diary—not this time though.

Now, she had some problems that she wanted me to help her with of a spiritual nature. She said she couldn't pay me at that time, but if I gave her my account details she would pay me as soon as she could. This is something I am always reluctant to do, even though I found myself saying yes and feeling strongly it was the right thing to do. Stated so, I helped her on numerous occasions over quite a few months.

Then one day early in 2015, Goldi messaged me saying, "Check your account please. I have paid you."

I did, and she had—totally unexpected. I had never once reminded her that she owed me money. I now see that as a test to see if I was ready to meet and work with Jillian.

But I digress. Goldi said she had some small gifts for me and would give them to a friend to hand them to me when her friend went back home to England from India. So, in the third week of May, I receive a phone call from Jillian asking if she could visit me at my home. Thus, on 29th May, I picked her up from the railway station and Jillian spent the afternoon with Anne and me. Now this is the remarkable thing about all this, I thought Jillian had known Goldi for many years, but she had only recently met her at a seminar that Jillian was giving in Delhi.

Therein, Goldi talked about me and how I had helped her. She then asked Jillian to take these gifts to me. So, even though Jillian and I live 130 miles apart, she agreed to do it. That said, Jillian had to catch three trains to reach me.

She said, "At first, I hesitated, realising we lived so far away; then at that time, not knowing anything about you, Alan, I found myself saying, 'Yes, I will take them to him'."

Indeed, Jillian thought I had known Goldi for many years as a close friend, which I had not, only as a client. Nonetheless, we all immediately became friends as if we had known each other for years. Thereafter, Jillian and I embarked on a new weekly radio show together called *Inspirational Voices* which can be listened to via my website. If, however, readers don't already know about this remarkable lady, they need to. After all, she is a true child of God put on this Earth to save many people. I am not exaggerating.

As mentioned previously, I have connections in the Hollywood film industry, so Jill asked me if I would ask my good friend, Cyrus Yavneh, about making her life story into a major film with me as a co-producer. Currently, we are at the stage of procuring investment (as of end of August 2016) to make the film. Also, Jill's story will be made into a stage play with David Parry as the producer/director—and me as his assistant.

Appendix 4
My Reality

I have tried to write a book no less than five times over the last decade; each time stopping after the first chapter and discarding my work. The difference this time is that the timing is right. I can understand now that I wasn't ready to tell my story beforehand. Indeed, over the last ten years so much has happened, which I have written about in this book. Undoubtedly, it's about having the right circumstances and influences in one's life that inspire one to achieve something important.

Now, my inspiration has come from three people. The first is Anne, my partner, who always supports me in everything I do. I am guilty, possibly, like so many others of not always appreciating what she does for me and other people. However, she certainly puts up with a lot from me and says being with me is like being on a permanent roller coaster ride. Indeed, she never knows where we will be, or what I will be doing next. Of course, each day brings new challenges that cannot be foreseen in our lives, but without them one does not grow as a person—and she recognises this. The next person who has influenced me to write is the author of Salem VI: Rebecca's Rising (the bestselling book), Jack Heath; a man who I feel so fortunate to have met and is now a friend. As such, he lives a busy life doing his daily radio show and running his business, while still finding time to write amazing stories. Hence, I thought if he is able to sit down and allocate time to write, then so can I. Certainly, it's about organizing one's day in a better way to allow time—which I never did before.

Now I come to the person who has had a major influence in my life; an influence making me realise that everything is possible if someone really wants to achieve something. Her name is Sherrie Wilkolaski. Without her belief that I could write this book and giving me a deadline to write it by, this book would not have been written. Her own work ethic is beyond reproach. Clearly, she works long hours each day, seven days a week, to help authors achieve their goals as well as creating amazing magazines.

So, when an opportunity presents itself in life, go for it. God puts people into our life for reasons. After all, he does listen to us and when the time is right for all parties, and then he can make things happen. Although, only if one grasps the moment and goes with it. Assuredly, never be afraid to follow your dream, even if it doesn't pan out exactly as expected. Either way, one hasn't wasted time or failed. Rather, one has found out something important about oneself: that one has the strength of character to move forward in life. Obviously, there are so many people who have wanted to do something important and have missed the opportunities through lack of belief in themselves.

Yet, as the saying goes, "It is better to have loved and lost than to never have loved at all."

This is true of all aspects of our lives, since we can never fail in life. After all, so-called failure teaches us about ourselves and life; so we always win. Nowadays, I see my life as an ongoing endless adventure of discovery; I wouldn't change anything because it is my journey, and even the negative things that have happened to me are just as important as the good things. All that has happened and still is happening to me is leading to my reality; my God. So, enjoy your journey, keep tuned in, and find your God.

Testimonials

Here is what clients of mine have to say about my work. This gives an insight to how bad spirit energies have affected some people.

From Sarra in London. 28 April, 2013.

Alan, I am not sure whether you remember me. I came to you via Internet in December because I was hearing voices. I ordered the package with you to help my family and myself, in order to release negative spirits. I am not sure what happened. In short, I have stopped taking my medication in January. I no longer hear voices; I am no longer paranoid, anxious or depressed. I have dumped my abusive partner of five years. My eldest brother who has always had anger management problems has calmed down. He no longer disrespects me when he talks to me. He has so much more confidence and strength in himself. He no longer seeks love or approval from my abusive mom. My brother now supports me emotionally and we are learning to know each other. Alan, I know you are responsible for my brother's change. Thank you so much.

I have known Alan Cox & his wife Anne for just a few months but they have become like friends to me. They are both tremendously supportive of the Norman Laud Association and even when not raising money for the Charity, constantly bring in goods for us to sell in our shop in Wylde Green in Sutton Coldfield.

The readings that Alan did at New Hall Hotel were extremely well attended and the feedback we received has been fantastic. On a personal basis, Alan has done readings for me and everything he told me has come true even down to my daughter getting a job when she was unemployed!

I would like to say thank you to Alan and Anne for their unstinting support and friendship.'

Sian Pemberton
Community Fundraiser
The Norman Laud Association

Message:

25/05/2010

Dear Alan

Just a quick thank you to you and Anne for coming and doing such fantastic spirit clearing in our home here in Newark. As a new property built in 2002, it's strange to think we needed it! The house feels completely different now with no cold spots and no rooms we don't like to enter anymore. As we discussed the most remarkable transformation happened to my Czech Au Pair. From a miserable, shy, pale, sullen girl she has become a lively friendly energised girl who is quite frankly unrecognisable from the person before your visit. We have all benefitted from your input. Long may it continue. With love and light.

Miche

I thought you would like an update following your visit to see me at Ginny's the other week. Firstly though, thank you for making the trip. I do not know if Ginny mentioned the fact that I was intrigued and apprehensive at the same time. I found the whole thing very enlightening and have discovered some differences in my life since. Firstly, prior to our meeting I felt

I was living a downward spiral and getting nowhere fast. Afterwards I found the complete opposite. Life seemed more positive and so did my business prospects. Maurice was quite a revelation to me. I do ask him to help me and to be with me. To start with, things were very lively and I started getting enquiries from the strangest of places which I can only attribute to 'his' work. My main concern is that I am finding it quite hard of late to 'connect' with him. It seems as though something is trying to 'block' me in some way. I hope not because Ginny reckons we work well together. For instance, I am petrified of heights. Last week I had to do a job that required me to climb a ladder. This is something I run away from whenever possible and was dreading the job. I continually asked for help and amazingly climbed the ladder, all most to the very limits of it not once but five or six times. The screw holes I drilled all lined up having asked Maurice to make sure they did and even to this day I have no concept as to why or how I managed to complete that job! Things on the house front seem to be falling in to place and so does Ginny's and my plans for the future. I still have some issues with that but hopefully they will be resolved. Interestingly enough, my ex-partner in Cardiff, is being nice to me!!! I am also aware of the recent help you gave Ginny. I find it absolutely amazing but it does work, I have seen it with my own eyes. Still leaves me feeling a little bewildered! One question though; is it right to ask for help to make your life financially secure? I don't mean by winning the lottery, but because of my disaster in Cardiff with my ex-partner, I want to rebuild my life and make it secure again, as I have done in the past. Well, thanks again to you both Ian (Case) PS Back has been OK since too!!!

I was lucky enough to be put in touch with Alan by another Psychic Surgeon south of the country as I was eager to find a Psychic Surgeon locally for issues with my eyesight experienced earlier this year. I sent Alan an email and he very promptly returned contact offering to see me at his home for a consultation as soon as possible.

I met up with Alan and his wife Anne soon after in their lovely home and I can only say that not only was the healing that he gave me first-rate and very effective, but also he is a very nice, knowledgeable and an extremely intuitive man, well connected to the Spirit World, and very much puts you at ease as soon as you put a foot through his front door.

Alan very modestly doesn't claim to have studied Reiki, or any healing art, let alone having attended any course, but let me advise you being someone myself who teaches Reiki healing, Alan's healing abilities are phenomenal. His connection to Spirit is very clear, strong, and he will demonstrate this by easily connecting to you and your guides. In fact Alan's abilities are beyond conventional healing systems.

Not only have I met a very talented Spirit Surgeon in Alan, but I have also made a true friend.

I would heartily recommend anyone to seek Alan's expertise.

Yours,
Alan Payne,

02/2010

I was put in touch with Alan and Anne after a yearlong search to discover the root only describe as a malevolent 'entity' would attack me on a regular basis. As well as all of this everything in my life was just wrong and had been for as long as I could remember.

Alan worked in a way I had never seen before—using his pendulum to detect and remove demons from different places and people in my life—who still had a pull on me and were dragging my energy levels down. About an hour into our session I went to the loo and on glancing in the mirror got the shock of my life. Looking back at me, was the me I had known about 10 years previously. The face of the girl I was before the nervous break-down, two divorces and current ill health!

Alan and Anne were with me for several hours, cleansing my past, the house and giving me hands-on-healing. When they left I felt what can only be described as 'light' and 'new'. It was as though I had been cleansed on every level and was starting out on a new page.

One week on I still feel so energised and light, I haven't been depressed from 3–7 pm, as I had been for the last year, my driving, which was slow from being dizzy has improved by miles (no pun intended) and I still have my 25-year-old face(?)!

I am waiting with anticipation for life to finally unfold. Thank you, Anne and Alan, for the vital energy and light you give where it is most needed. I will keep you updated…

L. Kilpatrick